SIMPLE PRAYERS
FOR A HECTIC LIFE

SIMPLE PRAYERS FOR A HECTIC LIFE

MAKING TIME FOR GOD IN YOUR LIFE

BY: P. C. DUKE

Copyright © 2008 by P. C. Duke

Cover design by P. C. Duke
Book design by P. C. Duke

All rights reserved.

No part of this publication may be reproduced without written permission of P. C. Duke.

For information regarding permission, contact P. C. Duke at pcduke48096@yahoo.com.

First Printing May 2009

ISBN – 978-0-578-02238-3

DEDICATION

This book is first and foremost dedicated to the Glory of God. During the writing of this book I felt more like the scribe than the writer. So many times I would find that the book was just writing itself right before my eyes. I would be obedient to God and start writing where I was led to. I freely thank our Father God for every word in this book.

ACKNOWLEDGMENTS

MY THANKS TO...

My thanks first go to our gracious Father, who without His gentle nudging this book would not exist.

Secondly, my thanks go to my loving husband; who without his unconditional love, support, and encouragement I would not be the person that I am today. His love has truly allowed me to blossom where I am planted.

Thirdly, I want to thank Dr. Sherill Piscopo of Evangel Christian Church in Roseville, Michigan. The first Sunday that I walked into Evangel Church she preached a sermon on trusting God. I have never forgotten that sermon. I was in a deep valley at that time in my life and her words helped me to understand that no matter how bad our circumstances may seem to us in the natural, God is in control of all things (even hurricanes). In His perfect timing, God will bring good out of whatever we are going through. Her sermon gave me perspective on how God works in our life that I had never known before and I have never forgotten.

Evangel Church has many good ministers and people affiliated with it. It was through Evangel that God led me to attend Destiny School of Ministry. Everything that was poured into me at Destiny, God took and put on these pages of this book. I also want to thank all of the excellent teachers that I have had while attending Destiny and especially the Dean, Dr. Rose Lafrenz. She truly has that rare ability to count it all joy no matter what obstacles are in her pathway and she does it all with a servant's heart and a smile. She has the patience of Job and the wisdom to graciously handle all situations presented to her.

Last but certainly not least, I want to thank Pastor Arnold Murray of Shepherd's Chapel in Gravette, Arkansas. Over the last 20 years plus, through his daily Bible studies, he has instilled in me and my family a love of the Word of God, verse upon verse, precept upon precept, line upon line. He has taught us how to rightly discern the Word of God and to be able to feast upon it.

INTRODUCTION

It is my sincere hope, for you the reader, that the lessons taught in these pages will help you to understand the how, when, where and why we need to pray to God; how to eliminate hindrances to your prayers and your blessings; and to understand how very precious you are to the Most High God.

TABLE OF CONTENTS

CHAPTER 1---WHY PRAY AND WHERE IS GOD ON YOUR TO DO LIST?...1

CHAPTER 2---THE NATURE OF GOD...3

CHAPTER 3---THE GOALS OF SATAN...10

CHAPTER 4---COUNT IT ALL JOY BY KEEPING YOUR EYES UPON JESUS...14

CHAPTER 5---WHY GOD WANTS A FULL CUSTODY RELATIONSHIP WITH YOU...16

CHAPTER 6---WE ARE ALL CHILDREN OF GOD...18

CHAPTER 7---WE ARE BLOOD BROUGHT...20

CHAPTER 8---HOW LUCIFER BECAME SATAN...22

CHAPTER 9---DON'T LET YOUR ANGER INVITE SATAN INTO YOUR HOUSE...24

CHAPTER 10---THE DIFFERENT NAMES OF SATAN...28

CHAPTER 11---SPIRITUAL WARFARE...30

CHAPTER 12---THE ARMOUR OF GOD...33

CHAPTER 13---I WILL BE YOUR GOD, IF YOU WILL BE MY PEOPLE...37

CHAPTER 14---GOD WILL DISCIPLINE THOSE WHOM HE LOVES…38

CHAPTER 15---INTO THE SMELTING POT WE GO…40

CHAPTER 16---THE HOLY SPIRIT…42

CHAPTER 17---GOD IS OUR TEACHER…47

CHAPTER 18---DON'T BE A "POOR ME BABY"…49

CHAPTER 19---THERE IS ONLY ONE UNFORGIVEABLE SIN…50

CHAPTER 20---AGREE TO DISAGREE…53

CHAPTER 21---DON'T SIT IN JUDGEMENT…56

CHAPTER 22---HOW TO FORGIVE UNFORGIVEABLE PEOPLE…59

CHAPTER 23---HOW TO FORGIVE REPEAT OFFENDERS WHO HAVE NO REMORSE…63

CHAPTER 24---WHY SHOULD WE FORGIVE?…66

CHAPTER 25---WHAT HAVE WE LEARNED AND WHY DO WE NEED TO PRAY?…67

CHAPTER 26---WHAT DOES GOD PROMISE TO US WHEN WE PRAY?…68

CHAPTER 27---WHEN AND HOW WILL GOD ANSWER OUR PRAYERS?…69

CHAPTER 28---WHY DOES IT SEEM THAT THE WICKED PROSPER?…71

CHAPTER 29---HOW DO WE GO ABOUT PRAYING TO GOD?...72

CHAPTER 30---PRAYING OVER SERIOUS SITUATIONS IN YOUR LIFE...77

CHAPTER 31---WHAT DOES SCRIPTURE SAY ABOUT CHILDREN?...84

CHAPTER 32---HOW TO PRAY FOR BADLY BEHAVING SPOUSES (YOU'RE NOT WITHOUT HOPE)...87

CHAPTER 33---HOW TO START RESTORING YOUR MARRIAGE...92

CHAPTER 34---LIFE CHANGES IN MEN AND WOMEN...95

CHAPTER 35---WHERE DOES GOOD NUTRITION FIT INTO A MARRIAGE?...99

CHAPTER 36---DIG INTO SCRIPTURE...103

CHAPTER 37---EDUCATE YOURSELF BY READING CHRISTIAN BOOKS ON MARRIAGE...104

CHAPTER 38---DON'T EVER TAKE YOUR SPOUSE FOR GRANTED...106

CHAPTER 39---PRAY WITH YOUR SPOUSE...108

CHAPTER 40---GOD HAS GIVEN US THE POWER TO BIND AND LOOSEN...117

CHAPTER 41---WHAT DOES GOD SAY ABOUT DIVORCE?...120

CHAPTER 42---BASIC PRAYERS FOR DAILY LIFE...123

CHAPTER 43---HOW TO PRAY USING THE BLOOD OF JESUS...127

CHAPTER 44---PRAYING OVER THE SICK...133

CHAPTER 45---PRAYERS TO BLESS OUR CHILDREN...140

CHAPTER 46---HOW CAN WE BE SURE WHAT THE WORD OF GOD SAYS?...145

CHAPTER 47---PRAYING OVER STRONGHOLDS...150

CHAPTER 48---HOW TO USE ANOINTING OIL FOR ADDITIONAL BLESSINGS?...153

CHAPTER 49---A BIBLICAL HANDLE FOR YOUR TEENS AND PRETEENS...157

CHAPTER 50---HOW TO TELL A GOOD MINISTER FROM A BAD MINISTER?...165

CHAPTER 51---HOW DO WE PRAY TO GOD WHEN WE HAVE REALLY SCREWED UP?...167

CHAPTER 52---DON'T WORRY, BE HAPPY OR COUNT IT ALL JOY...177

CHAPTER 53---WRITE THE VISION, HABAKKUK 2: 2...181

CHAPTER 54---WHAT DOES GOD SAY ABOUT FASTING?...185

CHAPTER 55---TITHING, DID I SAY TITHING?...187

CHAPTER 56---*"...For I will never leave thee, nor forsake thee"*, Hebrews 13: 5...190

CHAPTER 1

WHY PRAY AND WHERE IS GOD ON YOUR "TO DO" LIST?

Why pray? Who has the spare time to pray when we are so starved for time just to do the basics that we need to do to survive the day. If it's not running to the store for groceries, picking up the kids or dropping them off at music lessons or team practices; your day is spent in a constant sprint. You're always running; and let's not forget the orthodontist too, we as parents have logged in some quality time waiting for braces to be adjusted. All of these things are deserving of our time. Our spouse, our children and our families deserve quality time but what about God. Where does God fit into our day? How do we make quality time for Him?

Why pray? Doesn't God understand that I'm just too busy to pray right now? Isn't praying more for preachers and small children? Do regular adults really set time aside for God? Your answer should be a resounding yes. Scripture tells us that we should *"Pray without ceasing"* (1st Thessalonians 5:17); but how do we pray incessantly and still do everything that is required of us in a given 24 hour period and find just a little extra down time for the "me" part so you keep your sanity. These are all valid questions. You have to start by getting your priorities in proper order; God always first, spouse next, children third, your family fourth, and finally the rest of the world. Scripture teaches us in Matthew 6:33, *"But seek ye first the Kingdom of God, and His righteousness..."* Scripture further tells us *"In all ways acknowledge Him, and He shall direct thy paths"* (Proverbs 3:6).

Scripture tells us *"That I am the LORD thy God...Thou shall have no other gods before me"* (Exodus 20:2-3). Well, you might be thinking right now, "I'm okay on that one; I have no pagan altars set up in my house." You don't need a pagan shrine to worship at to have false gods in your life. A false god can be anything that you put before God. Some people obsess over their cars, homes, kids, spouse, jobs, pets, sports, soap operas, and the list goes on.

Think about where you place God on your "what's important" list. If you neglect your personal relationship with God, God will find a way to get your attention. You never, under any circumstances, want to put God in the position of having to clear the clutter of your life away for you to be able to focus on Him. Scripture tells us that "*I am a jealous God*" (Exodus *20*:5). He loves His children and wants an intimate relationship with each and every one of you.

If your placement of God is not first in your life it is very possible that you will always be a "Crisis Christian." A Crisis Christian will always have a crisis in their lives because that is the only way that God can get their attention and God wants you to talk to Him. He would rather you talk to Him on a regular basis. If your relationship is so distant that it takes God clearing the distractions out of your life to have you communicate with Him then God will keep you in a crisis to teach you the lessons that you need to learn so that you can grow in your faith. We all know people who could be called a Crisis Christian. When something goes wrong in their lives they try to do everything humanly possible to fix the situation and when all else fails they will resort to prayer because it can't hurt. They have tried everything else so they might as well see if God can do anything about this mess.

One additional thought here is that sometimes you will see people who find their way to God by going through a crisis. The crisis that they have endured has been the vehicle that has brought them into a personal relationship with Jesus Christ. After they have weathered the storm that brought them to God you will hear these same people using their crisis as an example of God's love and mercy to others in the same position as they were. These people will freely testify that they are thankful for going through what they did because without the experience they would not know God personally. They are counting it all joy (James 1:2).

CHAPTER 2

THE NATURE OF GOD

God does not cause bad things to happen to us. God by His very nature can do no evil. Scripture tells us that light can have no communion with darkness (2nd Corinthians 6:14). But, God will allow what will appear to us as bad things to happen to us to teach us lessons that we need to learn (see the complete Book of Job for an excellent example). God's Word does not come back void; it always comes back for His purpose and His pleasure, (Isaiah 55:11). No matter how dire things may seem to us in the natural world God is in charge of everything. Romans 8:28 declares this to us, *"And we know that all things work together for good to them that love God, to them who are the called according to His purpose."*

God wrote the rule book, HE is a supernatural God, He is the *"I AM THAT I AM"* (Exodus 3:14) which means that He is all things to all people at all times. To have a better understanding of *"I AM THAT I AM"* you need to know what the nature of God is.   Exodus 3:13-15 *"And Moses said unto God, Behold, when I come unto the children of Israel, and shall say unto them, The God of your fathers hath sent me unto you; and they shall say to me, What is His name? What shall I say unto them. And God said unto Moses, I AM THAT I AM: and He said, Thus shalt thou say unto the children of Israel, I AM hath sent me unto you."*

The Tetragrammaton is the sacred Hebrew word of four consonants. It can be transliterated YHWH, YHVH, JHWH, or JHVH. This stands for the infallible Name of God.   The name is usually transcribed in English as YAHWEH or JEHOVAH. What this means to us is that our God is everything to everyone. He is able to meet all of our needs no matter what they are. YHWH spans all verb tenses. It is the sacred revealed Old Testament Name of God.   Dr. Robert Costa Jr. (of Robert Costa Ministries) explains it this way: The "I AM THAT I AM" means "I AM

WHAT I AM AND I AM WHAT EVER I WANT TO BE." This name is often translated into the English versions of the Bible as the word "LORD" in all capital letters.

When you are reading the Bible you will see that the Name of God is used many times. It is important to know that each time that the Name of God is used the word God has a deeper meaning to it. The following is a very basic overview of what the Names of God are and in their definition you will find the true nature of God defined for you.

The name Jehovah means the unchangeable one, the revealing one and the intimate God.

He is our Jehovah Jireh which means that He provides for all of our needs. Genesis 22:14 *"And Abraham called the name of that place Jehovah-Jireh: as it is said to this day, in the mount of the Lord it shall be seen."* Jehovah-Jireh means our LORD will provide for us just as He provided manna and quail in the Wilderness to the Israelites. He also made their clothes and shoes to last the 40 years. He provided sweet clean water for them, brought them out of bondage, and kept them safe. Even when we are going through a valley in our life, our Jehovah Jireh has made a way for us to come safely through it. He is eternal and never changes.

Jehovah M'Kaddesh means the LORD my sanctifier. It also means that we are to set ourselves apart to be sanctified. God demands holiness from his children but holiness in itself is a choice that only we can make for ourselves. We are told that we are to be in the world, not of the world. God wants us to freely come to Him; He will never force us to choose Him. It is our free will choice always.

Exodus 17:15 *"And Moses built an altar, and called the name of it Jehovah-Nissi":* He is our Jehovah Nissi which means that He is the LORD our banner. He goes before us in battle and with Him we always have the victory. A good example of this is from Joshua chapter eight. Joshua sent men to take the city of Ai. Because they did not consult

God about their plans, their plans failed. When they repented of their sin against God and asked for His direction, they were victorious. We always need to consult God and ask Him for guidance before we act on things in our lives. Proverbs 3:5-6. *"Trust in the Lord with all thine heart; and lean not unto thine own understanding. In all thy ways acknowledge him, and he shall direct thy paths."* Biblically, a banner can also be a standard, a pole or a rod.

Exodus 15:26 *"And said, If thou wilt diligently hearken to the voice of the Lord thy God, and wilt do that which is right in His sight, and wilt give ear to His commandments, and keep all His statutes, I will put none of these diseases upon thee, which I have brought upon the Egyptians: for I AM the Lord that healeth thee."* He is our Jehovah Rophe which means the LORD that heals us. Repeatedly, throughout scripture we are told that God will heal us and it is His will that we are whole and healthy. Just from Matthew chapter eight we have numerous examples of Jesus healing people including Peter's mother-in-law, the centurion's servant and the man with leprosy.

Judges 6:24 *"Then Gideon built an altar there unto the Lord, and called it Jehovah-Shalom: unto this day it is yet in Ophrah of the Abi-ezrites."* He is our Jehovah Shalom which means the LORD our peace. The Bible gives us witness upon witness to the fact that if we keep our heart and mind on God we will have perfect peace in our life, no matter how chaotic our lives may be. If God is our center and focus we will be able to deal with whatever comes our way in a manner that is pleasing to God.

Psalms 23:1 *"The LORD is my shepherd; I shall not want."* He is our Jehovah Rohi which means the LORD is my shepherd, and we are His sheep. What does this mean to us? It means that our Father God, YAHWEH or Jehovah is whatever we need Him to be for us. He is our security and our trust. He is never changing. He is the maker of everything. He is ever present. He is unmade. He had no beginning and has no end. He knows all. HE IS. We are His sheep, and we know our master's voice.

Jeremiah 23:6 *"In His days Judah shall be saved, and Israel shall dwell safely: and this is His name whereby He shall be called, THE LORD OUR RIGHTEOUSNESS."* He is our Jehovah-Tsidkenu which means the LORD our righteousness. Scripture tells us that we should strive to have a righteousness that is from God in our lives. Proverbs 14:34 *"Righteousness exalteth a nation: but sin is a reproach to any people."*

Ezekiel 48:35 *"It was round about eighteen thousand measures: and the name of the city from that day shall be, The LORD is there."* He is our Jehovah Shammah which means the LORD the present. God's presence is all around us. Scripture tells us from Matthew 28:20 *"...lo, I am with you always, even unto the end of the world."* We find our rest in God's presence, we find our shelter in God's presence and we find our peace in God's presence. In Joshua 1:5 God tells us *"...I will be with thee: I will not fail thee, nor forsake thee."*

Jehovah Tsebaoth means The LORD of Hosts. Because we are children of God we have the right and authority to call upon His Hosts when we need to. Psalm 103:21 teaches us, *"Bless ye the LORD, all ye His Hosts; ye ministers of His, that do His pleasure."* Most people just think of the "Hosts" of God as His ministering angels but that is not true. There are many examples throughout Scripture that show angels are just one type of Hosts. Some others would include the stars, the sun, the moon, the weather, birds, animals and the Host of Saints.

Jehovah Makkeh means the LORD who molds and corrects me. God with His Word wants to mold and shape us so that we can have a personal relationship with Him and live a life that is pleasing to Him. His molding and shaping of us is not in a punitive form but instead it is a loving correction. We need to have a contrite and humble heart for God to be able to mold and shape us. Psalm 51:16-17 says to us that *"For thou desirest not sacrifice; else would I give it: thou delightest not in burnt offering. The sacrifices of God are a broken spirit: a broken and a contrite heart, O God, thou wilt not despise."* It is a continual, life long process where we are cleaning out the stuff in our lives that is worldly and replacing it with what pleases God.

Jehovah Gmolah means the LORD who rewards. Hebrews 11: 6 teaches us *"But without faith it is impossible to please Him: for he that cometh to God must believe that He is, and that He is a rewarder of them that diligently seek Him."* Jehovah Gmolah will reward our good or Godly behavior and He will likewise reward our ungodly behavior. There are consequences to all of our actions, be they good or bad. Jehovah Gmolah will see that we all get what we deserve.

Jehovah Elohay means the LORD My God. Jehovah Elohay shows Himself to us as our personal God whom we should call upon when we find ourselves in the midst of trials.

El-Elohe-Israel means the personal God of Israel. El-Elohe is the personal God that we can call upon to petition God on behalf of others going through trials.

Jehovah Eloheenu means the LORD our God. When the Body of Christ as a whole entity is under attack then Jehovah Eloheenu is the personal God that we can call upon to bring the Body through the trial.

El Elyon means The God Most High. Psalm 7:17, *"I will praise the LORD according to His righteousness: and will sing praise to the Name of the LORD Most High."*

Elohim means the Sovereign, Mighty Creator. Elohim is a plural Hebrew word which is used in Genesis chapter 1 verse 1, *"In the beginning God created the heaven and the earth."* It gives witness to the Trinity of God, The Father, The Son Jesus Christ and the Holy Spirit. It also means the God who makes covenants with His people. In the Bible it is used 2,700 times.

El Shaddai means the All Sufficient one. He is the God who supplies our needs abundantly so that we have blessings that are more than enough.

El Shaddai is our God who gives us our supernatural miracles. He is able to take our negative situations and supernaturally turn things around to our advantage.

Adonai is our LORD and Master. It is another plural word which gives a witness to the Trinity of God, The Father, The Son Jesus Christ and the Holy Spirit. Our personal relationship with God should be willingly as a bond servant to his master. A bond servant is a slave who has the choice of going free, but of their own free will chooses to stay a servant.

The names and definitions that I have given you are just the basics on the subject. Scripture teaches us in Hosea 4:6 that *"My people are destroyed for lack of knowledge...."* I highly recommend that you take the time to read Pastor Marilyn Hickey's book *"The Names of God"*. It will enrich your relationship with God by going into detail on the meaning of all of the Names of God. This book will amaze you and greatly bless you. I also highly recommend that you seek out Appendix 4 of *"The Companion Bible"* by Dr. E. W. Bullinger *"The Divine Names and Titles"*. There are plenty of newer versions of *"The Companion Bible"* but the 1909 version from Dr. Bullinger is the best.

Now that you know the nature of God, you can better see that all evil in this world comes from the devil. How can I say that God does not cause evil? Number one, it is not in His nature; we only have to go back to the light can have no communion with darkness scripture (2nd Corinthians 6:14) or even James chapter 3:11, where it speaks that bitter waters and sweet waters cannot come from the same well. Number two, God has given each and every person a free will and what does that mean to us? It means that God did not want a bunch of people running around this world who could only worship Him twenty-four hours a day.

What good is it when someone says to you, "I love you" if they have no choice. Love that is forced has no value. Love that is freely given is priceless. So God gave us a free will to do good with or to do bad with. God gives us a free will to choose to walk after His ways or to walk outside of His ways. Deuteronomy 11:26-28 teaches us, *"Behold, I set before you this day a blessing and a curse; A blessing, if ye obey the commandments of the LORD your God, which I command you this day: And a curse, if ye will not obey the commandment of the LORD your God, but turn aside out of the way which I command you this day, to go after other gods, which ye have not known."* Satan influencing man's free will choice is the source of all evil in this world.

CHAPTER 3

THE GOALS OF SATAN

John 10:10 teaches us that the thief (Satan) comes for three purposes; to steal, to kill, and to destroy your happiness any way that he can. Further breakdowns of these goals are:

(1) Satan continually strives to keep people from accepting the Gift of Salvation that is offered to us by Jesus' crucifixion.
(2) He continually strives to prevent believers in Jesus Christ from growing and maturing in their faith so that they can walk in their purpose for the Kingdom of God.
(3) He continually strives to cause a believer to turn away from God and start serving him. He comes at you with spiritual attack after attack to try to dishearten you from your belief in God. He will make you question if a personal relationship with God is really worth everything that you are going through.

How does Satan accomplish these goals? One of his most powerful tactics is convincing Christians that he and his demons don't exist. Scripture tells us that my people perish for lack of knowledge (Hosea 4:6).

His most powerful tactic is convincing us that we are powerless over him. Scripture teaches us: *"Behold, I give unto you power* (meaning: authority) *to tread on serpents and scorpions, and over all the power of the enemy: and nothing shall by any means hurt you"* (Luke 10:19). Pastor Kenneth E. Hagin gives us a deeper understanding on this subject in his book, *"The Believer's Authority":*

> In speaking about "serpents and scorpions," Jesus is talking about the power of the devil---demons, evil spirits, and all his cohorts. We need to realize that we've got authority over them!

> Does the Church of the Lord Jesus Christ have (or need) any less authority today than it had in the first century? It would be preposterous to think so, wouldn't it?
> The value of our authority rests on the power that is behind that authority. *God Himself is the power behind our authority! The devil and his forces are obliged to recognize that authority!*
> The believer who thoroughly understands that the power of God is backing him can exercise his authority and face the enemy fearlessly.
> What is authority?
> *Authority is delegated power.* [1]

Once again, in Matthew 28:18, *"And Jesus came and spake unto them, saying, All power* (again, meaning: authority) *is given unto me in heaven and in earth."* Pastor Hagin continues teaching us in Matthew 28:18.

> When Christ ascended, He transferred His authority to the Church. He is the Head of the Church, and believers make up the Body. Christ's authority has to be perpetuated through His body, which is on the earth. (Throughout Ephesians and elsewhere in the epistles, Paul uses the human body as an illustration of the Body of Christ).
> Christ is seated at the right hand of the Father---the place of authority---and we're seated with Him. If you know anything about history, you know that to sit at the right hand of the king or the pope means authority. We died with Christ, and we were raised with Him. This is not something God is going to do in the future; He already has done it! [2]

If we are ignorant of the tools that God our Father has given us to have power over Satan and all powers of darkness then we forever remain ignorant of who we are in Christ (Colossians 1:27). Because of our

---

[1] Hagin, Kenneth E.; The *Believer's Authority* (Tulsa, Oklahoma: Kenneth Hagin Ministries, 1986), p. 7.

[2] Hagin, p. *11*.

ignorance of God's Word and our ignorance of the inheritance that we have through The Blood of Christ (Revelation 12:11) we are rendered powerless over him.

Satan is the father of all lies; he is so good at his job that he can even twist Holy Scripture to deceive you. The Gospels of Matthew 4, Mark 1 and Luke 4 all give accounts of the devil trying to tempt Jesus when He was in the Wilderness. Don't ever be fooled on this subject, the devil knows Holy Scripture much better than you or me and every chance that he can, he will tempt all of us to sin.

Even with that being said, you still cannot truthfully use "the Devil made me do it" as an excuse for why we sin. Sin is a choice that we freely make. If we "blame out" by saying someone else made me mad or made me do something that I didn't want to do then we are giving control of our emotions away. NO ONE makes you do anything. It is YOUR free will and choice how you choose to react and yours alone. So always take responsibility for YOUR actions, be they good or bad.

We are all going to make mistakes in our flesh bodies. It is how we handle them and if we learn from our mistakes that matters. Our mistakes have the ability to teach us more than all of the sermons in the world. Also learn how to say "I was wrong" and "I'm sorry", it goes with being an adult and accepting responsibility for our actions. If you can say that you won't need it because you don't make mistakes then you are not being truthful with yourself and others. 1st John 1:8-9, *"If we say that we have no sin, we deceive ourselves, and the truth is not in us. If we confess our sins, He is faithful and just to forgive us our sins, and to cleanse us from all unrighteousness."*

I repeat: God cannot do evil; it is not in His nature. He will allow us to go through trials and tribulations to strengthen us, grow us in our faith and to clean the garbage out of our lives (James 1:2-4). Every one of us has a purpose to serve in the Kingdom of God. We all make up the Body of Christ on this earth. Each of us is gifted by God with different talents and abilities to be used in building His Kingdom. No one of us is more important than the other (1st Corinthians, chapter 12).

CHAPTER 4

COUNT IT ALL JOY BY KEEPING YOUR EYES UPON JESUS

Why pray? James 1:2 tells us to count it all joy; 1st Thessalonians 5:18 further declares, *"In everything give thanks: for this is the Will of God in Christ Jesus concerning you."* Right now that may seem pretty hard to do, but keep in mind, God will pull good out of what seems to be a bad situation, in His perfect timing. His Word declares it as so in Genesis 50:20, *"But as for you, ye thought evil against me; but God meant it unto good, to bring to pass, as it is this day, to save much people alive."*

A true example of this is a lady was broadsided at an intersection. She was taken to the hospital to be checked out. She was so badly banged up from the impact of the accident that you could see the brand of the car imprinted upon her chest and a lot of other bumps and bruises. When the doctors initially examined her they found a dangerously low white blood count and this made them look at her closer. The closer that they looked at her, the more invasive testing they ordered. Finally, after ten days in the hospital, they gave her a diagnosis. The doctors told her that she was lucky to be alive; and in their opinions she would have been dead within the week from her untreated dangerously high blood pressure and consequently failing kidneys if there had been no medical intervention. God pulled good from what most people would have perceived as evil.

You may be thinking how can I count it all joy when the price of gas is teetering around 4 dollars per gallon, your 9th grade son just announced to you that he sees no need for further education because he knows everything that he needs to know to be successful in life, the budget this month did not include the water heater leaking and no one is due for a pay raise in your family for another six months. It's not easy but you need to keep your eyes focused upon Jesus. Our Father God knows that life in the natural is not easy for us. So when we stay focused on thanking Him, praising Him and also praying for other people's needs no matter what is happening in the natural He sees this as a sacrifice on our part and as such honors it in this way. Hebrews 13:15 teaches us, *"By Him therefore let us offer the sacrifice of praise to God continually, that is, the fruit of our lips giving thanks to His name."*

When we put others first this is having a servant's heart. A servant's heart in us pleases God very much. Remember, Jesus Christ Himself set the example for us by washing the feet of The Twelve in John, chapter 13 and in that time period the job of washing other people's feet would normally have fallen upon the lowest servant or a slave. God knows each and every need and want that we have no matter how well hidden they may be to the world. Matthew 6:8, *"... for your Father knoweth what things ye have need of, before ye ask Him."* When we set aside ourselves and selflessly put other people's needs first God, will take care of both of the needs.

CHAPTER 5

WHY GOD WANTS A FULL CUSTODY RELATIONSHIP WITH YOU

Why pray? Because God's Word tells us repeatedly "when you pray" not if you get around to it, scripture emphatically says "when." So what is praying? Praying is your spoken words or thoughts to God; it is just talking to Him in your regular language. Praying can also just be singing to Our Father a song that praises Him. Praying or prayers do not have to be fancy words or a specific prayer or prayers that you learned by rote as a child. The only prayer in the whole Bible that we are officially told to pray is that of "The Our Father" in Matthew 6:9-13.

Every other prayer in every other prayer book has been made up by someone in a flesh body. Now there is nothing wrong with praying in this manner but put yourself in God's place just for a moment. You are "THE FATHER" of the whole universe. You want a personal relationship with each and every child of yours, but each time your child comes before you to speak, they recite the same words. If your children said the same formal speech to you every time they spoke to you what sort of relationship do you think you would have? You would know that child, but not very well. You would have a fast food sort of relationship. Yes, it does meet the basic requirements for a meal but it really doesn't nourish your body well.

You may be thinking right now "I go to church every Sunday, isn't that enough talking to God, what more does He want out of me, doesn't He realize just how busy I am?" God knows what you are doing every second of everyday; and the truthful answer is no, it is not enough. God wants more than just "visitation rights on Sunday"; He wants a full custody relationship. Each and every one of us needs an intimate, personal relationship with Jesus Christ. Every day, each of us makes a decision as to what type of relationship that we are going to have with God. We can have a fast food drive through type of relationship with

God which results in our barely knowing Him. Or we can have a seven course, sit-down meal at the fanciest restaurant type relationship with God which gives us a deep intimacy with Him.

It's the same thing for God, when you come before Him and just go through a litany of rote recitations, it does not encourage the deep and intimate relationship that Our Father God longs for with each of His children. God's Holy Word warns us that this type of prayer (vain repetitions) is offensive to God (Matthew 6:7). You are precious in His sight, you are the apple of His eye, and He wants to know you and He wants you to know Him as your ABBA FATHER.

The term ABBA FATHER is used by Jesus in the Garden of Gethsemane (Mark, chapter 14) to address His Father. It is an Aramaic word that denotes the intimacy that is between a small child and his father. It is a very close relationship word that only a child who felt safe, secure and loved by his father in their relationship, would use. In English it is comparable to a little child saying daddy. If He cares enough about you to number the very hairs on your head (Matthew 10:30 and Luke 12:7), I think it is safe to say everything about you is of concern to Him. He wants you to walk in your full inheritance in Him. Sadly, unless you take time to communicate with Him it will never happen.

CHAPTER 6

WE ARE ALL CHILDREN OF GOD

God views all of us, no matter how old we are as His children and this is what His Word teaches us on this subject. *"But who so shall offend one of these little ones which believe in me, it were better for him that a millstone were hanged about his neck, and that he were drowned in the depth of the sea"* (Matthew 18:6). His Word repeats this warning to anyone who comes between His relationship with His children and Himself in Mark 9:42 and Luke 17:2.

God's feeling towards us, His children, is further viewed in Mark 10:13-16. *"And they brought young children to Him, that He should touch them: and His disciples rebuked those that brought them. But when Jesus saw it, He was much displeased, and said unto them, Suffer the little children to come unto me, and forbid them not: for of such is the kingdom of God. Verily I say unto you, Whosoever shall not receive the Kingdom of God as a little child, he shall not enter therein. And He took them up in His arms, put His hands upon them, and blessed them."*

God loves His children so much that He gave each and every one of us a guardian angel. Matthew 18:10 confirms this for us, *"Take heed that ye despise not one of these little ones; for I say unto you, That in heaven their angels do always behold the face of my Father which is in heaven."* Furthermore scripture tells us in Psalms 91:11-12, *"For He shall give His angels charge over thee, to keep thee in all thy ways. They shall bear thee up in their hands, lest thou dash thy foot against a stone."* There should be no doubt in your mind how much your Father God loves you and how precious you are in His sight; and therefore, how much it hurts Him when we choose to disobey Him in sin.

God takes His role as Our Father very seriously and this is why He views us, His children as sheep. Sheep always need someone to take care of them and protect them so God has given us a good shepherd.

That good shepherd is Jesus Christ His Son. *"I am the good shepherd: the good shepherd giveth His life for the sheep"* (John 10:11). *"My sheep hear my voice; and I know them, and they follow me: And I give unto them eternal life; and they shall never perish, neither shall any man pluck them out of my hand. My Father, which gave them me, is greater than all; and no man is able to pluck them out of my Father's hand. I and my Father are one"* (John 10:27-30). It's important that we pray to God, but it's equally important that we also listen for His response to that prayer. The above scripture says *"My sheep hear my voice"*, you will learn to recognize the voice of God. God communicates with His children in different ways. Some people will tell you that they can audibly hear the voice of God. Others will say that they just know when God tells them something. God also will communicate through dreams and visions.

It doesn't matter what method God uses to speak to you, if He wants to say something He will make Himself known to you. The most important lesson to be learned here is to listen to him *and* listen for Him to speak. The more you pray and communicate with God, the closer He will come to you (James 4:8). The closer you come to Him and grow in your relationship with Him, the better you know Him and the more He speaks to you. It's a win-win situation, you become a better person because you are closer to God and God is happier because His child has a deep, intimate relationship with Him.

CHAPTER 7

WE ARE BLOOD BROUGHT

God loved us so much that He sent His Son, Jesus Christ into this world to be crucified upon the cross so that we might have eternal life with Him (John 3:16). You need to fully realize that He loves us so much that if you or I were the only one alive on this earth He still would have let Jesus be crucified upon the cross at Calvary for you. In the book, *Blessing the Next Generation,* by Pastors Marilyn Hickey and Sarah Bowling they further explain what Jesus' death upon the cross should mean to us as believers.

> When we accept Jesus as our Savior, we are acknowledging with our will and our faith that Jesus' death on the cross -- the only sacrifice necessary for us to be forgiven of sin -- was for us personally. All God requires of us is to believe in what Jesus did, believe He is the Son of God, and receive Him as the one who saves us from eternal death and gives us eternal life.
>
> This is the heart of the born-again experience, the way in which we receive a new spirit and a new nature. The real person deep inside us is changed the instant we accept Jesus Christ as our Savior. We are forgiven completely and we are given everlasting life (John 3:16). The Holy Spirit becomes available to us as never before and we become *fully able* to live a godly life. The slate is clean -- we are in right standing with God, and therefore, in position to establish right things in our lives.
>
> We then must make a decision with our will and by faith to follow and obey Jesus as our Lord. We are empowered to do this because Jesus sends the Holy Spirit to help us to live righteously.[3]

---

[3] Bowling, Sarah and Hickey, Marilyn; *Blessing the Next Generation* (New York, New York: Faith Words, Hachette Book Group, 2008), p. 40-41.

Upon the cross Jesus Christ made six statements. In John 19:28 we find Jesus' fifth statement from the cross, *"I thirst."* He was then given a sponge dipped in wine vinegar and held to His mouth. J. W. Shepherd in his book, *"The Christ of the Gospels"* gives us further insight into this:

> Jesus received the vinegar for a purpose. His parched lips and throat would not render clear articulation until thus moistened. His senses now revived, He uttered the final redemptive words: "It is finished!" The work of redemption, which was the object of His earthly life, had been completed and the plan of salvation established. The prophecy with reference to the Messiah has been realized and the last suffering for sin endured. Nothing has been left undone or unborne. It was a shout of triumph. He cried with a loud voice, not the weakened utterance of one dying from physical exhaustion but of a Conqueror in the full flush of strength and victory. His task was complete.[4]

His final words are found in John 19:30, *"It is finished."* This was a Greek business term *(tetelestai)* used to signify a paid in full, debt discharged transaction. This is what it means when Holy Scripture says that we are blood brought. Jesus' blood was spilled on the cross to pay the price for the sins of the world. 2nd Corinthians 5:21 says, *"For He hath made Him to be sin for us, who knew no sin; that we might be made the righteousness of God in Him"* and further 1st John 1:7 states, *"... and the Blood of Jesus Christ His Son cleanseth us from all sin."* When Scripture says that by His stripes we were healed, it means that all diseases and sins were covered under His precious shed blood. His blood being shed is what paid the price for these infirmities to be healed in us even today (1st Peter 2:24 and Isaiah 53:5) and our sins to be forgiven.

---

[4] Shepherd, J. W., *The Christ of the Gospels* (Grand Rapids, Michigan: Eerdmans Publishing Co., 1946), p. 603.

CHAPTER 8

HOW LUCIFER BECAME SATAN

What is the true nature of Satan; he is pure unadulterated evil. Scripture tells us in Isaiah 14:12-13, *"How art thou fallen from heaven, O Lucifer, son of the morning! How art thou cut down to the ground, which didst weaken the nations! For thou hast said in thine heart, I will ascend into heaven, I will exalt my throne above the stars of God: I will sit also upon the mount of the congregation, in the sides of the north: I will ascend above the heights of the clouds: I will be like the Most High."* To better understand the importance of why we pray you need to have a clear understanding of what you are warring against in this world when you pray.

Before Satan fell from God's Grace and took a third of the angels with him (Revelation 12:4), he was a being that brought God much pleasure. Ezekiel 28:14-15, *"Thou art the anointed cherub that covereth; and I have set thee so: thou wast upon the holy mountain of God; thou hast walked up and down in the midst of the stones of fire. Thou wast perfect in thy ways from the day that thou wast created, till iniquity was found in thee."* At that time Satan's name was Lucifer which means "bright morning star". His only job in heaven was to constantly sing God's praises. After a while Lucifer became prideful and started to believe that he could become an equal to God. You can see from the aforementioned scripture quote from Isaiah just how prideful and puffed up he became. These "I Will" statements from Satan illustrate just how much his heart had turned from God.

Pastor Billye Brim explains it like this in her book *"The Blood and the Glory"*.

Lucifer's five treasonous *"I Wills"* reveal much.

- *"I will ascend into heaven."* His kingdom was in a place from which he had to go up to carry out his rebellious plan.

- *"I will exalt my throne above the stars of God."* Lucifer had a throne, and therefore a kingdom.
- *"I will sit also upon the mount of the congregation, in the sides of the north."* This describes the place of God's throne. Lucifer was after the throne of God.
- *"I will ascend above the heights of the clouds."* The atmosphere of Lucifer's kingdom included clouds---clouds he would surmount in an attempt to exalt his throne. Many Bible scholars agree that his kingdom was here on earth. It was "the world that then was."
- *"I will be like the Most High."* All this entails we do not know. But his later temptation of Jesus reveals that he wanted to receive rather than to give worship.

There was a real "Star Wars"!

Lucifer deceived even some of the angels and led an organized revolt against the Most High God.

What was the outcome?

Jesus told us. *"And He said unto them, I beheld Satan as lightning from heaven" (Luke 10:18).*

I believe Lucifer's rebellion so angered God that He removed Himself from the environs of earth sending it into a chaotic wasteland covered with dark water.[5]

---

[5]Brim, Billye; *The Blood and the Glory* (Tulsa, Oklahoma: Harrison House, Inc., 1995), p. 26-27.

CHAPTER 9

DON'T LET YOUR ANGER INVITE SATAN INTO YOUR HOUSE

Satan is called by many different names in the Holy Bible. The reason for this is each name that he is called has a different meaning and it is usually describing what he is doing or how he is doing it. He is also the master of counterfeiting. In the end times he will skillfully try to pass himself off as Jesus Christ and a lot of people will be taken in by his con. Even now, he and his fallen angels (demon spirits) will try to trip you up by twisting the truth to deceive you.

Deception is one of the major currencies that Satan uses as he operates in this world. Strife, revenge, pettiness, dissention, anger, and distrust are just some of the negative emotions that Satan employs against us each and every day to get us caught in his snare. There are times that we all get mad, frustrated or exasperated at a person or a situation. Is it okay to get angry with this? A qualified yes to the question; it all depends upon how we handle our anger. God's Word in Ephesians 4:26-27 teaches us: *"Be ye angry, and* (meaning - "but") *sin not: let not the sun go down upon your wrath: Neither give place* (meaning- "opportunity") *to the devil."*

When we choose to react with anger, afterwards we need to calm down and ask God to forgive us for our outburst. Secondly, we need to give our anger with the given situation or the person to God to deal with it for us. If we hold on to the anger and don't ask for forgiveness or forgive the source of the anger, than we, as such, are opening the door to our house and asking the devil to come in and make himself at home for an extended stay with us.

We are basically setting an extra plate at our table, pulling out our best tablecloth, napkins, silverware, bed sheets and asking him to make himself comfortable for the long haul. Anger sets us up to walk in sin and disobedience to God. Satan feeds off anger and any other negative emotion that we have in our lives. Nothing pleases Satan like our choosing to disobey God and holding onto the anger in our life.

Then how do we know if we are sinning with our anger or not? Try asking yourself a couple of questions regarding your anger. Are you consumed by it, is it all you can think about all day long, each and every day? Is your anger blinding you from thinking straight? Is your anger keeping you from being happy? Is your anger making you a bitter person? A yes to any of these questions is not good. Anger is not the only emotion that can cause you to sin. We have learned that there is a time and a place where anger is not wrong.

What about righteous indignation? Sometimes we should be angry. It is just and right to be angry. Look at the example of Jesus cleaning out the temple from the moneychangers in Matthew 21:12-13 and John 2:13-16. Jesus was angry at how the temple had been disrespected. Pastor Arnold Murray of Shepherd's Chapel in Gravette, Arkansas says it this way, "Christians are not milk toast type people. We are passionate about this gift of life that God has given us. We should live life to the fullest. We are children of the Most High God; we have the best in life because that is the legacy and inheritance that Our Father God has given us."

In Revelation, chapter 3, God is speaking to the Church of the Laodiceans. In verses 15 and 16, He expresses His disgust with them: *"I know thy works, that thou art neither cold nor hot: I would thou wert cold or hot. So then because thou art lukewarm, and neither cold nor hot, I will spew thee out of my mouth."* There is nothing wrong with expressing our emotions passionately. With that said though, I have to add caution here; any emotion that we have can be taken to a place of excess where it becomes a sin.

We have all seen people who after a loved one has died, five years later they are still so deep in grief that they are practically immobilized. Satan will take our human weaknesses and use them to his advantage. Satan can and will pervert anything that is good and wholesome and turn and twist it into negative, unhealthy emotions. If you are still unsure if your given reaction is Godly or not, ask God for wisdom and discernment so that you can learn from this experience and go forward with your life.

I have heard some people say to me, "If it doesn't directly affect me, why should I care". There are times in our lives where you have to take a stand for what is right and confront evil. The issue may not be directly impacting you today or tomorrow but as the 17th century conservative Edmund Burke is attributed with saying *"All that is necessary for evil to triumph is for good men to do nothing"*. There are going to be times in all of our lives that we will encounter people that do not have the ability to speak for themselves and they will need us to speak up in their defense. These people may not directly impact me today or even tomorrow but it is the right thing to do, to champion them and their issues.

We all have to decide where we stand on the issue of right and wrong. It is not always comfortable to be standing up for character, morals and values in our society but if you are a child of God you will do the right thing no matter what the cost is to you. There are some issues and wrongs in this life that should make our blood boil with righteous indignation; just like when Jesus threw the moneychangers out of the Temple. With that said, turn your righteous indignation into something positive and be a person who brings about change for the good. One person can make a difference. Righteous indignation does not mean you are in sin, but do not let it turn to anger.

If you are a child of God, you will have the courage of your Godly convictions to stand on to right the wrong. One only need look as far as Washington D.C. to see politicians that have prostituted their morals and values for power, position and money. Their souls are for sale as much as a prostitute sells their body. You will often times see these same people making headlines when their immoral activities are exposed. The real shame of it all is that our culture will treat these morally bankrupt people as if they are celebrities and worthy of praise.

Look at the fight that has gone on in the courts of this land just to keep the Ten Commandments in the public arena. There are actually schools that have been forced to take them out of the classrooms because the courts in their state are afraid that the children might look at them and be influenced by them. Twenty years ago that lack of logic would have been unthinkable. Then you will have people scratch their heads in wonderment as to the how and why that we have some of the ungodly laws that we do. But they are just too lazy to be bothered to stand up for what's right and voice their opposition to evil.

Many people define happiness as having an adult beverage in one hand, chips in the other and a game or a soap opera on the T.V. They don't want to be bothered. God expects us to be the difference makers in this world, we are the head not the tail, we are above not beneath (Deuteronomy 28) and we are to be the salt and light of this world (Matthew 5:13-14). When we walk in the Spirit of God, then God endows us with a spirit of boldness that will enable us to walk outside of our comfort zone. We never want God to say of us that we are neither hot nor cold therefore I will spew you out of my mouth (Revelation 3:16).

CHAPTER 10

THE DIFFERENT NAMES OF SATAN

In Revelation 9:11 he is called Abaddon which is the Hebrew name for Satan and it means destruction. In the same scripture he is also called Apollyon which is the Greek word meaning destroyer. Additionally in this same scripture he is also called the Angel of the Bottomless Pit. In Revelation 12:10 he is called the Accuser. In 2nd Corinthians 11:14 he is called Angel of Light because he transforms himself into one, to deceive people. In 1st John 4:3 he is called the Antichrist because he will deceive people by pretending to be Jesus in the end times.

In Revelation 14:9-10 he is referred to as the Beast. This is another name that the Bible says he will be called in the end times. Matthew 12:24 calls him Beelzebub which means the Ruler of the Demons. In 2nd Corinthians 6:15 he is called Belial which is the demon associated with wickedness and guilt. In Revelation 12:9 he is called the Deceiver, the Great Dragon and the Serpent of Old, the Devil (also see 1st John 3:8) and Satan (Mark 1:13). In Matthew 13:39 he is called the Enemy and in John 17:15 he is called the Evil One.

In John 8:44 he is called the Father of Lies and a Murderer and in 2nd Corinthians 4:4 he is called the God of this Age. In Isaiah 14:4 he is called the King of Babylon, and in Ezekiel 28:12 he is called the King of Tyre. Leviathan is what he is called in Isaiah 27:1 and in 2nd Thessalonians 2:8-10 he is called the Lawless One. In Daniel 8:9-11 he is called the Little Horn (horns symbolize power in the Bible) and in 2nd Thessalonians 2:3-4 he is called the Man of Sin.

Colossians 1:13-14 calls him the Power of Darkness, and in Ephesians 2:1-2 he is called the Prince of the Power of the Air. In Ephesians 6:12 he is called the Rulers of the Darkness, and in Luke 11:15 he is called the Ruler of Demons. In John 12:31-32 he is called the Ruler of this World, and in 2nd Thessalonians 2:3-4 he is called Son of Perdition. In

Revelation 9:1 he is called a Star fallen from heaven to the earth. In Matthew 4:3 he is called the Tempter and in John 10:10 he is called the Thief. In Ephesians 6:16 he is called the Wicked One.

1st Peter 5:8 says to us: *"Be sober, be vigilant; because your adversary the devil, as a roaring lion, walketh about, seeking whom he may devour."* Maybe this one scripture sums up Satan and the different roles that he plays to try to deceive us as well as any could. All of the above names that Satan is called define different ways and means that he tries to use against us to cause our soul to be eternally damned. If you allow yourself to be caught up in one of Satan's snares then you will be consumed by "your adversary the devil" who does "walk about as a roaring lion" just looking for those that "he may devour".

In Galatians 5:19-21 we can further see a fuller listing of what Satan has brought to this earth. *"Now the works of the flesh are manifest, which are these: Adultery, fornication, uncleanness, lasciviousness, idolatry, witchcraft, hatred, variance, emulations, wrath, strife, seditions, heresies, envyings, murders, drunkenness, revellings, and such like: of the which I tell you before, as I have also told you in time past, that they which do such things shall not inherit the kingdom of God."* This pretty much covers all that is evil in our world: past, present, and future. The secular world refers to these as the Seven Deadly Sins: lust, gluttony, greed, sloth, wrath, envy and pride.

CHAPTER 11

SPIRITUAL WARFARE

When we pray we just don't bring our petitions, cares and concerns to our Father. An equally important aspect of praying is Spiritual Warfare. How do we conduct Spiritual Warfare? Very basically by praying and singing the praises of God to God. Dr. Lester Sumrall in his book *Take It...It's Yours, Seizing Your Spiritual Dominion* speaks to the power that we have in praising God.

> Jesus said, *"Whatsoever ye shall bind on earth shall be bound in heaven: and whatsoever ye shall loose on earth shall be loosed in heaven...For where two or more are gathered together in my name, there am I in the midst of them"* (Matthew 18: 18-20).
> The devil is subject to the believer's *faith,* and he cannot overcome it.
> The devil is subject to the believer's *authority,* and he must submit to it.
> The devil is subject to the believer's *rights,* and he can't take them away.
> The devil is subject to the *words* a believer speaks, and he must obey. If the believer tells the devil to go, he must go!
> One of the most dramatic and powerful demonstrations of dominion is *singing...*
> God wants us to be glad and sing songs of victory. Go throughout life singing, "Jesus already has won! The Church already is victorious!"[6]

Part of Satan's punishment for his prideful act of disobedience in heaven was that God took what was Lucifer's job in heaven and used it against him as punishment. So when you sing or just listen to what ever type of praise music that you like, you are silencing the devil and you put him

---

[6] Sumrall, Dr. Lester, *Take It...It's Yours, Seizing Your Spiritual Dominion* (South Bend, Indiana: Lester Sumrall Evangelistic Association, 1986), p. 85-86.

on the run from you and your family. James 4:7 teaches us to *"Submit yourselves therefore to God. Resist the devil and he will flee from you."*

How is Spiritual Warfare officially defined? Spiritual Warfare is also a spiritual battle that Satan and his demons wage against those who believe upon Jesus Christ and His teachings. Spiritual Warfare is a battle that Christians wage against Satan through prayer. This can be broken into two types of prayer: Intercessory and Warfare Prayer.

Intercessory Prayer is when you directly petition God to intercede into a given situation that is of concern to you. Warfare Prayer is when we directly rebuke Satan in the Name of Jesus Christ. We come against him and all of his evil works or plans that he has for us. It is very important to keep in mind that in both types of prayer we should always say them in "The Name of Jesus Christ". This is witness to our professing our belief in Jesus Christ and His confession of faith. Finally, Spiritual Warfare is a battle directly between God's Angels and Satan's demons; this one does not involve us directly but we are still involved because it is a battle that is being fought over us.

Let's clarify here, what is the above mentioned confession of faith that Jesus spoke of. And understand that this is not said to offend any religious denomination. Facts are just that ... *"facts"*, and as such do not have an agenda to offend anyone but to state the truth. There are additional examples of the truth of this but I stayed with the simplest of the explanations.

In Matthew 16:18 we see Jesus addressing this: *"And I say unto thee, That thou art Peter, and upon this rock I will build my church; and the gates of hell shall not prevail against it."* When you analyze the verb tense of Petros (Peter) and Petra (this rock) you find that Petros is of the masculine gender and Petra is of the feminine gender. Petra denotes an immovable rock or cliff. Petros is the Greek translation of Kephas, a stone, which was Peter's name in Aramaic which refers back to the "Bar-jona" part of his name (which means son of Jona – John 1:42).

Petra, this rock, the confession of faith, is what Jesus was professing to build His church upon; it is not Peter the man who God built His church upon, but rather His confession of faith.

In Matthew 16:15-16 we further see that, *"He saith unto them, But whom say ye that I am? And Simon Peter answered and said, Thou art the Christ, the Son of the living God."* Since Petra is feminine it must refer to a feminine noun expressed or implied. That noun would logically be Homologia, which means a confession; and it was Peter's confession that was the subject of the Father's revelation and the Son's confirmation. Finally in Matthew 16:17, *"And Jesus answered and said unto him, Blessed art thou, Simon Bar-jona: for flesh and blood hath not revealed it unto thee, but my Father which is in heaven."*

"Facts are stubborn things; and whatever may be our wishes, our inclination, or the dictates of our passions, they cannot alter the state of facts and evidence."

~~~ John Adams (2nd President of the United States), in defense of the British Soldiers on trial for the Boston Massacre ~~~
December 4, 1770

CHAPTER 12

THE ARMOUR OF GOD

Ephesians 6:10-17, *"Finally, my brethren, be strong in the LORD, and in the power of His might. Put on the whole armour of God that ye may be able to stand against the wiles of the devil. For we wrestle not against flesh and blood, but against principalities, against powers, against the rulers of the darkness of this world, against spiritual wickedness in high places. Wherefore take unto you the whole armour of God that ye may be able to withstand in the evil day, and having done all, to stand. Stand therefore, having your loins girt about with truth, and having on the breastplate of righteousness; And your feet shod with the preparation of the gospel of peace; Above all, taking the shield of faith, wherewith ye shall be able to quench all the fiery darts of the wicked. And take the helmet of salvation, and the sword of the Spirit, which is the Word of God."*

Things that we think of as traditional weapons won't do a thing to hurt Satan and the other angels (which are now called demons) that chose to disobey God. That is why God gives us His armour, so that we are protected from Satan as we wage war on him.

"The Girdle of Truth" means that we must know and keep close to us at all times, the truth of God's Holy Word. The truth of the God's Word is that our salvation is in Jesus Christ alone. "The Breastplate of Righteousness" means the right doing of Jesus Christ, not ours. Even when we do our best it is never equal to the best of Jesus Christ (Isaiah 64:6). God knows how hard we try and consequently how far we fall from the goal.

God does not call us to be perfect. He calls us to be FAITHFUL. *"His lord said unto him, well done, thou good and faithful servant: thou hast been faithful over a few things, I will make thee ruler over many things: enter thou into the joy of thy lord"* (Matthew 25:21). Being faithful to

Our Father God means that each and every day doing our best with a heart full of love for God and showing that love to each other. God knows we will never be perfect in this flesh body but He will honor our efforts and it pleases Him greatly when we try our very best to be obedient children to Him.

"The Shoes of the Preparation of the Gospel of Peace" mean that we are to be ever ready to explain why we have faith in Jesus Christ. Hebrews 11:6, *"But without faith it is impossible to please Him: for he that cometh to God must believe that He is, and that He is a rewarder of them that diligently seek Him."* This means that we need to daily study God's Holy Word.

It is also very important that we try to memorize a little bit of Holy Scripture each and every day. This way all the little pieces that we learn will add up each day so that we are making ourselves stronger in the LORD every day. Think of it as exercising a muscle. You start with a small amount of exercise and gradually build up to a daily amount of exercise that will keep your body healthy. The more that we learn of God from His Holy Word the closer that we will come in our relationship with Our Father God, *"Draw nigh to God, and He will draw nigh to you"* James 4:8.

"The Helmet of Salvation" means that we are to protect our thoughts from Satan. The blood that Jesus Christ shed upon the cross protects our minds. When we keep our focus upon Jesus, He will keep our hearts and mind in perfect peace (Isaiah 26:3). Philippians 4:7 further states for us, *"And the peace of God, which passeth all understanding, shall keep your hearts and minds through Christ Jesus."*

"Our Shield of Faith" is only as strong as our faith in God is. 2nd Corinthians 5:8 tells us *"For we walk by faith, not by sight."* Faith is our believing that God is who He says He is and that He is capable of doing all that He has said He will do (Hebrews 11:6). Romans 10:17 tells us that: *"So then faith cometh by hearing, and hearing by the Word of God."* We strengthen our shield of faith by feeding daily on the Word of God.

"The Sword of the Spirit" is the Word of God. *"For the Word of God is quick, and powerful, and sharper than any twoedged sword, piercing even to the dividing asunder of soul and spirit, and of the joints and marrow, and is a discerner of the thoughts and intents of the heart"* (Hebrews 4:12). 1st Peter 1:25 further teaches us, *"But the word of the LORD endureth forever..."* When you speak the Word of God to anything evil that comes against you, the Word of God becomes your two edged sword. Satan does not want any part of your Sword of God's Word. He cannot stand against the Word of God.

Our Father God also gives you songs of praise to fight the devil with. When you sing songs of praise to God, Satan wants no part of you. He hates to hear God praised, especially since that was his old job in heaven. When you are having a really bad day if you start singing God's praises in song or if you just put on music that praises God you will set the devil running. *"Submit yourselves therefore to God. Resist the devil, and he will flee from you"* (James 4:7).

You will find if you try this, that it is very hard to stay in a bad mood when you are singing God's praises. If you look at Psalm 47:6-7 you will find that we are told to sing praises to God; *"Sing praises to God, sing praises: sing praises unto our King, sing praises. For God is the King of all the earth: sing ye praise with understanding."* There are many more places in Holy Scripture that we are told to sing praises to Our Father.

Ephesians 6:12 teaches us that *"For we wrestle not against flesh and blood, but against principalities, against powers, against the rulers of the darkness of this world, against spiritual wickedness in high places."* What does all of this mean to us? God sent Jesus into this world so that His death upon the cross would redeem us from the curse of death that Adam and Eve's act of disobedience in the Garden of Eden had brought upon us.

Jesus came into this world so that we might have abundant life on this earth and everlasting life with God in eternity (John 10:10). Satan came to try to take that life away from us in any way that he can. For a more complete study on Spiritual Warfare you may want to read: *Spiritual Warfare* by C. Peter Wagner, *Silencing the Enemy* by Robert Gay, and *Spiritual Warfare* by Derek Prince.

CHAPTER 13

I WILL BE YOUR GOD, IF YOU WILL BE MY PEOPLE

When we pray, we are coming against the active works of the devil both in our daily life and in all of his plans to steal our future happiness away from us by catching us in his snares. When we pray, we are bringing our petitions to God to ask Him to make a way for His Will in our lives. When we pray, we are asking God to intervene for us in all of our situations. When we pray, we are asking God our Father for the favor that we as a child of God deserve; and we as a child of God have a full inheritance to the covenant promises that He made with Abraham.

This is called The Abrahamic Covenant and it is found in Genesis 12:1-3. *"Now the LORD had said unto Abram, Get thee out of thy country, and from thy kindred, and from thy father's house, unto a land that I will show thee: And I will make of thee a great nation, and I will bless thee, and make thy name great; and thou shalt be a blessing: And I will bless them that bless thee, and curse him that curseth thee: and in thee shall all families of the earth be blessed.*" For a deeper study on this subject read Genesis chapters 12 through 22.

God's Holy Word says to us in Jeremiah 7:23, *"But this thing commanded I them, saying, Obey my voice, and I will be your God, and ye shall be my people: and walk ye in all the ways that I have commanded you, that it may be well unto you."* Again in Jeremiah 30:22, *"And ye shall be my people, and I will be your God."*

CHAPTER 14

GOD WILL DISCIPLINE THOSE WHOM HE LOVES

God in His ultimate wisdom will sometimes use whatever pleasure that we took in a sin and turn it around so that it becomes our worst nightmare. A very basic example of this would be a spouse who decides they want a divorce. When they get the divorce that is going to make everything perfect in their lives, they find out they have made a grave error. The problem wasn't with the marriage, it was with themselves. This is used as a teaching lesson to us and some of us need more examples of what not to do than others. The Israelites wandering around the desert for 40 years is a good example of God's justice. They wandered in that desert until all of the generation that disobeyed Him had died.

When you find yourself wandering in your own wilderness, you need to ask God for the wisdom to understand what He wants you to learn from it. Remember too, that when we find ourselves in said wilderness or a valley this is the time that God expects us to be growing in maturity in our faith walk with Him. Keeping Him lifted up in praise and worship will help the time that you spend in your valley to go faster. It will also help you to be more cheerful during this time and thank Him for seeing the undeveloped value in this lump of clay that we call ourselves.

God will freely grant us wisdom if we just ask it of Him. In James 1:5 we learn: *"If any of you lack wisdom, let him ask of God, that giveth to all men liberally, and upbraideth not; and it shall be given him."* Don't forget that He also tells us that you have not because you ask not. You can find witness to that in the following scriptures: Matthew 7:7-8, Matthew 21:22, Luke 11:9-10, John 14:13-14, and John 16:23-24.

I thought, "God will ALWAYS forgive us…" doesn't He? Yes, God in His ultimate mercy and grace forgives His children when WE ASK for forgiveness. God's Word teaches us in Matthew 6:14-15, *"For if ye forgive men their trespasses, your heavenly Father will also forgive you: But if ye forgive not men their trespasses, neither will your Father forgive your trespasses."* Additionally Matthew 7:1-2 further teaches us, *"Judge not, that ye be not judged. For with what judgment ye judge, ye shall be judged: and with what measure ye mete, it shall be measured to you again."*

God will forgive us and show mercy unto us only as much as we show forgiveness and mercy to other people (Matthew 18:21-22, Luke 17:3-4). But that said, God will allow us to deal with the consequences of our actions to teach us additional lessons that we need to learn to grow and mature in our faith. Our Father God is not punitive, but He is a just God. Scripture teaches us: *"As many as I love, I rebuke and chasten: be zealous therefore, and repent"* (Revelation 3:19).

To discipline a child is not abuse; it is an act of love. Never discipline a child when you are angry, take time to calm down and ask God for wisdom before handing out a punishment of any sort. Take the time to explain to your child why they are being disciplined; make this a teachable moment in your child's life. Discipline should always be just, even-handed, fair and never punitive. Revenge should have no part of Godly discipline. God's Word further states in Proverbs 13:24, *"He that spareth his rod hateth his son: but he that loveth him chasteneth him betimes."* Once again in Proverbs 29:15, *"The rod and reproof give wisdom: but a child left to himself bringeth his mother to shame."*

CHAPTER 15

INTO THE SMELTING POT WE GO

You need to think of the trials and tribulations that we go through daily as the smelting fire of life. This is one of the jobs of the Holy Spirit to clean us up. He is called the Spirit of Burning in Isaiah 4:4 because His cleansing fire will burn off the junk in our lives. We need to humbly come before God and tell Him to do whatever it takes to purify us and to keep us, even when our flesh bodies don't want any part of being kept.

One of the outward signs that the Holy Spirit is actively house cleaning for us can be that we will start crying for no apparent reason. Listening to Christian Worship Music can sometimes do this for us and it is the evidence of the Holy Spirit working within us. In our flesh bodies we have a lot in common with precious metals. Precious metals like gold and silver need to be put into a smelting pot and have the slag cooked out of them. In their natural state they may not look very pretty or even show any hint of their true value. But after they have been heated in the fire and all of the impurities in them are cooked out, what you have left is of great value.

Trials and tribulations are our personal smelting pots and they clean out the slag in our lives. If you are not tested then how will you ever grow in your faith walk with God? 2nd Corinthians 5:7 says: *"For we walk by faith, not by sight"*. Romans 10:17 further states, *"So then faith cometh by hearing, and hearing by the Word of God."* James 1:2-4 teaches us, *"My brethren count it all joy when ye fall into divers temptations; Knowing this, that the trying of your faith worketh patience. But let patience have her perfect* (meaning: "mature") *work, that ye may be perfect and entire, wanting nothing."*

Some of us, more than others, need a show and tell from God; we need the dots connected for us. A lot of us have to be in a total crisis situation (in our own personal smelting fire) in our life before we realize that nothing that we can do in the natural is going to have an impact upon changing our situation. At this point we usually start communicating very well, and often, with God.

CHAPTER 16

THE HOLY SPIRIT

The Holy Spirit or the Holy Ghost is the third person of the Godhead. Scripture gives witness to this in Matthew 28:19, and 2nd Corinthians 13:14. He is fully God just as the Son and the Father are. His personal characteristics of both a will (1st Corinthians 12:4-11), and a mind (Romans 8:27) show that He has a distinct personality. Additional traits include that The Holy Spirit speaks in Revelation 2:7 and in Romans 8:26, *"Likewise the Spirit also helpeth our infirmities: for we know not what we should pray for as we ought: but the Spirit itself maketh intercession for us with groanings which cannot be uttered."*

The Holy Spirit is responsible for helping us to find the words that we need when we pray. He gives our words a heartfelt elegance so that what is in the depths of our hearts comes pouring out to God in prayer. You will find yourself praying in words that you never even imagined were possible to come from your tongue. When the Holy Spirit convicts your heart, everything that has been hidden away in your heart will be wrung out of you in your special prayer language. You may even be surprised to find yourself in tears as you pray to God.

Speaking in tongues is an evidence of being baptized in The Holy Spirit. Some people will not believe that speaking in tongues is anything more than just made up jibberish. If you have truly been baptized in the Spirit you will not question this, because the issue will be settled in your heart and you will have the peace that passes understanding in your heart (Philippians 4:7). This is one of those areas that people hold very passionate varying views on; don't argue this point with people. If they truly have their mind set with a certain opinion, just agree to disagree. An argument that you will hear presented in regards to speaking in tongues is: if this is real then why didn't Jesus speak in tongues? For a good answer to that question I am going to quote Dennis and Rita Bennett's book, *The Holy Spirit and You:*

> Some say: "That's right! Jesus didn't speak in tongues when he was empowered by the Holy Spirit, so why should we?" It is true that Jesus did not speak in tongues, but He said that we would do so. Jesus did not need the edification of speaking in tongues, and there were no barriers in His soul that made it necessary for His Spirit to speak to the Father in a language His mind did not understand. Indeed it is impossible to imagine Him doing so. Moreover speaking in tongues is the manifestation that was to come at Pentecost in "the fullness of time." We have already seen that it was when Jesus went back to be with his Father in Heaven, that the Holy Ghost could then be given in His fullness, which in turn made speaking in tongues possible. Jesus had said: "The things that I do, you will also do, and you will do greater things, because I am going to My Father" (John 14:12). The ability to speak in languages we have learned, then, could be seen as part of the "greater things" that Jesus said we would do after He had gone back to Heaven.[7]

You may be wondering how you can receive the Baptism of the Holy Spirit. I am going to continue with a little more from Rita and Dennis Bennett to help answer your question.

> You have received Jesus as your Savior, you have renounced any false teachings that might hold you back or confuse you, and now you're ready to pray to be baptized in the Holy Spirit. Who is going to baptize you in the Holy Spirit? Jesus is going to do it! This being so, you can receive the Holy Spirit anywhere, anytime, can you not?

---

[7] Bennett, Dennis and Rita, *The Holy Spirit and You*, (Gainesville, FL: Bridge-Logos, 1998), p. 75.

"But I thought someone had to lay hands on me to 'give' me the Holy Spirit." No, we have already settled that. Because you have received Jesus, you already have the Holy Spirit, so no one needs to "give" Him to you, even if they could! Jesus is living in you, and He is ready to baptize you in the Holy Spirit as soon as you are ready to respond. Having someone lay hands on you may be a help, and it is certainly scriptural, but not absolutely necessary.[8]

If you have not personally experienced the baptism of the Holy Spirit just prayerfully and reverently ask the Holy Spirit to come into your heart and baptize you with His Spirit. Sometimes people will immediately start speaking in a totally developed spiritual language. Other times your special prayer language will develop just like our natural language skills, a little at a time. This is a very personal experience and everyone will be just a little bit different. You will know it when the Holy Spirit fills you up. There is no mistaking it when the anointing of the Spirit of God falls upon you.

I personally find that when I am in a situation where the anointing of the Holy Spirit is so very high upon me I feel as if my batteries have just been recharged and nothing can stop me I am just so full of energy. If I am coming back from a church service in the evening, it will be four or five hours before I am even able to think about sleep. I am just too buzzed up on the Spirit of God. You just feel wonderful and that all is well in your world. It's really a fantastic feeling.

The Holy Spirit is able to be impacted by personal actions: He may be grieved (Ephesians 4:30), He can be lied to (Acts 5:3), and He may be blasphemed to (Matthew 12:31-32). The Holy Spirit has Divine characteristics: He is eternal in nature (Hebrews 9:14); He is omnipresent, meaning He is present in all places at all times (Psalm 139:7-10); He is omnipotent, meaning having unlimited authority or influence (Luke 1:35); and He is omniscient, meaning having infinite

---

[8] Bennett, Dennis and Rita, The *Holy Spirit and You*, (Gainesville, FL: Bridge-Logos, 1998), p. 53.

awareness, understanding, insight, and complete knowledge (1st Corinthians 2:10-11).

The Holy Spirit has different names such as: The Holy Spirit (Luke 11:13), The Spirit of Grace (Hebrews 10:29), The Spirit of Burning (Isaiah 4:4), The Spirit of Truth (John 14:17), The Spirit of Life (Romans 8:2), The Spirit of Wisdom and Knowledge (Isaiah 11:2), The Spirit of Promise (Ephesians 1:13), The Spirit of Glory (1st Peter 4:14), The Spirit of God and of Christ (1st Corinthians 3:18), and The Comforter (John 14:16).

The Holy Spirit is the member of the Trinity that dispenses the Gifts of the Spirit. The Gifts of the Spirit are different God given abilities that we are to use for the Glory of God (1st Corinthians 12:14-26). The Holy Spirit decides who gets what gift or gifts (1st Corinthians 12:1-12; 28-31; Romans 12:6-8). The gifts fall into three groups: church leadership, speaking and service to others. The gifts are without repentance which means that once they are bestowed upon a person they will not be taken back no matter how they are used. If you use the gifting that you receive responsibly and in a manner that brings honor and glory to God, He is pleased and will bless you with more gifts. If you don't make honorable use of your gifting then God will deal with you on this subject in His own time.

We find the listing of the purpose of the gifting in Ephesians 4:12-15. Basically you can sum up their purpose by saying, the gifting that we, as the Body of Christ receive, are to edify the Body of Christ and to grow the Body of Christ. We can find the fruit of the Spirit in Galatians 5:22-23, they are, *"But the fruit of the Spirit is love, joy, peace, longsuffering, gentleness, goodness, faith, meekness, temperance; against such there is no law."* This is just a short list of who the Holy Spirit is and what He does. For a more complete study of the Holy Spirit and to learn more about your spiritual gifting, I highly recommend you read *Holy Spirit Today* by Dennis and Rita Bennett, *Your Spiritual Gifts* by C. Peter Wagner and *Holy Spirit Baptism* by Don Basham. All three are excellent books.

CHAPTER 17

GOD IS OUR TEACHER

The trials and tribulations that we go through in our lives is a continual learning process where in God is our teacher and we are the student. Isaiah 54:13 speaks to our educational training from God, *"And all thy children shall be taught of the LORD; and great shall be the peace of thy children."* If your attention is on everything else instead of God, then God will do whatever He needs to do, to get your attention. When He finally has your undivided attention, then and only then, can He start to help you grow in your faith, so that you can grow in your relationship with Him.

Here again, we are taught to count it all joy because no matter how bad things may seem to us in this natural world, God has a plan and a purpose for every trial that He allows us to go through. You need to be mindful that for every trial and temptation that we go through God in His wisdom has already made a way for us to come through it safely. A really good example of this is when Abraham was told by God to take his only son Isaac and offer him as a burnt offering to God (Genesis 22:2). Now Abraham did as he was told to do by God, he didn't know how God would save the boy but he knew God would. He was so sure of this fact that in Genesis 22:5 he says to the servants that accompanied him and Isaac, *"...Abide ye here with the ass; and I and the lad will go yonder and worship, and come again to you".* His deep and abiding faith in God told him that somehow God would make everything all right once again.

Isaiah 55:11 confirms this for us: *"So shall my Word be that goeth forth out of my mouth: it shall not return unto me void, but it shall accomplish that which I please, and it shall prosper in the thing whereto I sent it."* Ultimately, after each testing that we go through we should have learned a lesson from it and we should find ourselves closer to God after this. Trials and testing are to help us be stronger in our faith so that as we grow, we are better able to serve Him and to help His Kingdom grow on this earth. This is all part of our maturing in our faith process and our wholeheartedly being in submission to the Will of our Father God. If we daily submit to the Will of God, then we will walk in His blessings and we will speak His blessings from our mouth.

CHAPTER 18

DON'T BE A "POOR ME BABY"

Don't ever give the excuse that you can't pray to God because He is mad at you and won't listen to your prayers. When you make a statement like this, it is nothing more than being a "Poor Me Baby." God loves you and don't ever doubt it. Can God be disappointed in your actions? Yes, God can be very disappointed in His Children when they disobey Him. 1st Corinthians 10:13 says it like this: *"There hath no temptation taken you but such as is common to man: but God is faithful, who will not suffer you to be tempted above that ye are able; but will with the temptation also make a way to escape, that ye may be able to bear it."* Further more in James 1:12 we have this statement on temptation: *"Blessed is the man that endureth temptation: for when he is tried, he shall receive the crown of life, which the LORD promised to them that love Him."*

If you truly feel that God is angry with you, then it is time for some very overdue and serious, one on one time with your Father. Come before Him in all reverence, love, submission, and with a contrite heart; surrender to Him. Ask Him, if you have offended Him and if you have for Him to show you the error of your ways. Ask Him for forgiveness and wisdom. Ask Him for mercy. I repeat: God loves you; He wants the best for you always. He will not turn His back on you. Hebrews 13:5 confirms this: *"...I will never leave thee, nor forsake thee."*

When we are walking in sin, the sin separates us from God. 2nd Corinthians 6:14 confirms it for us, *"... for what fellowship hath righteousness with unrighteousness? And what communion hath light with darkness?"* If your free will choice to sin has built a wall between you and Our Father then tear it down. We are told repeatedly in Scripture that if we ask forgiveness of God, He will grant it to us. It just takes us to ask, what are you waiting for?

CHAPTER 19

THERE IS ONLY <u>ONE</u> UNFORGIVEABLE SIN

You need to know that there is only one unforgivable sin that is mentioned in the Bible. You will find it in Matthew 12:31-32, *"Wherefore I say unto you, All manner of sin and blasphemy shall be forgiven unto men: but the blasphemy against the Holy Ghost shall not be forgiven unto men. And whosoever speaketh a word against the Son of Man, it shall be forgiven him; but whosoever speaketh against the Holy Ghost, it shall not be forgiven him, neither in this world; neither in the world to come."* Mark 3:22-30 gives a second account of this.

Theologians have many different ideas on exactly what blasphemy of the Holy Spirit is. I think it is safe to agree that basically blasphemy is the vile insulting of God, or in any way showing a lack of respect for God by our actions and spoken or written words. While we are here, it is critical that you are familiar with Galatians 6:7, *"Be not deceived; God is not mocked: for whatsoever a man soweth, that shall he also reap."*

You never under any circumstances want to ever mock God. I would not want to be in your shoes if you do. It's a dangerous place to be, because our God will not tolerate it in any way, shape or form and it's an incredibly foolish thing to do because our Father is a just God. If you choose to mock Him or show Him disrespect in any way He will deal with you in His own way and timing.

Here is an example of why you should not be mocking God in any way or at any time. A man and his son delivered newspapers to 400 customers each and every day. They worked from 1 a.m. to about 6 a.m. every day, seven days a week to deliver these papers. On a cold and rainy Thanksgiving morning the father had a flat tire. This put him about two hours behind schedule. At the family's Thanksgiving dinner the man foolishly said to God while saying grace "thanks for the lovely flat tire, I really enjoyed it." His daughter rebuked him for making such a statement to God and he did sort of take it back but you could tell that he was still angry with God over his flat tire.

The next night he and his son left their home to go and deliver the papers again. Well this night the father got flat tire number two. The next night the father had car troubles. The next night nothing happened to the father but as he was coming home after he had delivered his portion of the papers he noticed that his son's papers were not delivered yet and there was no reason that he should have been this late. It turned out that his son had ended up in a ditch trying to avoid hitting an animal.

He was unhurt, the car was totaled and this was a time period that cell phones were expensive and uncommon. The ditch was one of those very large county drainage ditches that normally would have had a large amount of water in it. This night it was bone dry and the car fit into it neatly. Now, I would not say for sure that God allowed these things to happen to this man and his son but this lesson is one of those things that this man and his family have never forgotten and this man has never spoken in a disrespectful manner to God again.

God is in control of all areas of our life. He can either bless our life or allow it to be cursed. It is our free will choice what we choose. Scripture confirms this for us in Deuteronomy 11:26-28, *"Behold, I set before you this day a blessing and a curse; A blessing, if ye obey the commandments of the LORD your God, which I command you this day: And a curse, if ye will not obey the commandments of the LORD your God, but turn aside out of the way which I command you this day, to go after other gods, which ye have not known."*

Proverbs 18:21 tells us that, *"Death and life are in the power of the tongue: and they that love it shall eat the fruit thereof."* We will never know how many unpleasant experiences we avoid when we ask God to bless us and to give us His favor in our lives. This is another reason why we should always ask God for His traveling mercies and that He blesses our journey before we drive out of our driveways. God is interested and concerned about every aspect of our lives, even that we arrive safely at our destination and home again; no matter if it's cross country or just across the street.

To get back to blasphemy of the Holy Spirit, these are some of the explanations given as to what blasphemy of the Holy Spirit means. There is the school of thought that says that you can not commit it unless you are one of "The Elect of God" and you refuse to allow the Holy Spirit to use you to witness to Satan in the end times. Others feel it is if you refuse to accept the offer of salvation from Jesus Christ, and if you refuse this you also refuse God's gift of forgiveness so therefore you are unforgivable. Still others strongly feel that it has to do with anyone who mocks the works of the Holy Spirit with the intent of keeping others from following Jesus Christ.

This is one of those highly charged religious subjects that you would be best served to do your own in depth study upon and come to your own Biblical conclusion. As long as you stay away from disrespecting the Holy Spirit in any way, shape or form you should be alright. I have my own personal opinion on which explanation I think is the correct one but bottom line it is not a religious issue that you should argue about with anyone.

CHAPTER 20

AGREE TO DISAGREE

There are some things we are just not going to know what the correct answer is until we meet Jesus in person. Therefore and especially, if it is not a salvation issue, never argue over it. There are a lot of deeply religious people, good decent people, who love God dearly but they drive people (especially family members) away from God. They are so convicted that their denominational belief system on anything Godly is the only way to believe that if you don't agree with them then you are on your way to hell in a hand basket. Just to make sure I am being painfully clear on this subject, the hand basket here is one woven of your evil deeds.

There are many Biblical points that people feel very strongly about, a very good example of this is the subject of "The Rapture". Many people feel that The Rapture is not mentioned in scripture but just as many others will swear on a stack of Bibles that we are all going to be raptured up. This is one of those subjects that we need to show respect to each other's opinions on, rather or not it is part of our belief system.

The important thing to take from this whether or not you agree with the Rapture Theory is this question: is your heart right with God? Have you asked Jesus to come into your heart? Have you accepted Him as your personal LORD and Savior? Have you asked God to forgive your sins? Have you told Him how sorry you are for those sins? Have you told God how much you love Him?

If you have a personal relationship with God, and you are doing your best to be an obedient child to Him with your heart in full submission to Him, then you are also most likely in the Will of God for your life and are pleasing Him. Remember, He doesn't call us to be perfect because it is impossible for us to do so; He calls us to be faithful and obedient children. Most importantly, He asks that the love that we give Him is of our own free will. He doesn't want our love if it is coerced in any way from us. It has to be truly given from our heart to our Father to have any value and when it is freely given, and only then, is it a priceless gift to Him.

Another point here that supports not arguing over religious issues is that in the European Middle Ages, people wasted scads of time arguing over how many angels could fit upon the head of a pin and dance upon the head of a pin. Remember, arguing of this type is a "time waster" and it opens the door for Satan. There is a time, when debating a subject has merit, but select your battles carefully so that your conduct brings honor and glory to our Father God, not Satan. There is nothing wrong with agreeing to disagree.

If you happen to have more Biblical knowledge than someone that you are speaking with, be careful that you do not abuse the person with lesser knowledge. You can inadvertently turn someone away from God if you over load their thinking. Use caution with those that are not at the same level as you are; we have all been beginners at some point in our life. We are to be diligent in our seed planting but it is up to God to determine at what rate the plant grows and when it takes root. So handle with extreme care those who are new or newer to God's Word.

In regards how to handle a situation when you sincerely believe that a person's belief system is going to lead them to eternal damnation this is what I recommend. First, calmly and in a friendly and concerned manner sit down with them and explain to them why you believe they are mistaken in their belief. Don't be surprised if they do not agree with you but at least you have logically and lovingly presented to them what you believe to be the truth on the topic. Ephesians 4:15 speaks to this subject matter: *"But speaking the truth in love..."*

This is where you probably come to a point in your conversation where you most likely will agree to disagree and that's okay. By not acting in a pushy and offensive manner, you are still keeping your relationship with said person intact. This consequently will allow you to keep a good rapport with them so that they still would feel safe with you in further discussing the topic at any time.

You never want to shut the doorway to communications. It's not your job to hit people over the head with your Bible. We all know people who act "holier than thou" and it is very offensive. The best way that you can proceed is to prayerfully give these people over to God, to deal with. Acts 9:18 says, *"And immediately there fell from his eyes as it had been scales: and he received sight forthwith, and arose, and was baptized."*

The Holy Spirit is the only one who is able to convict a person's heart, and God is the only one who is able to remove the blinders of ignorance from a person's eyes. Just keep interceding for this person in your prayers and God is faithful to answer your prayers. No good will come out of the situation if you push the issue and cause the person to back into a corner with their wrong beliefs. All you achieve in this would be that the person would have to keep defending their beliefs just to save face, even if they might be thinking about changing their mind.

CHAPTER 21

DON'T SIT IN JUDGEMENT

On a personal level God seems to put a lot of people in my life that are either hard-core atheists or agnostics. The agnostics seem to take the attitude that "something" must be up there but they really have no clear idea what it might be, and at this point in their lives they have no real interest in finding out for themselves. The first reaction that I get from these people when they find out that I am a Minster of God is they think that they can't talk to me. They quickly get very defensive expecting me to try to force my beliefs upon them and expect me to tell them that they are hell bound.

When I don't verbally assault them after a while and with some friendly conversation they let a little of their defensive wall down when they figure out that I am not going to force my beliefs upon them. I instead try to befriend them and give them a safe person to speak to without judgment. I keep these people in my prayers and I do wholeheartedly believe that the Holy Spirit will convict their hearts. This again is a good example of how we can plant and water a seed, but only God can make it grow.

There are many examples of atheists who set out to disprove God's existence only to end up believing in Him. It seems the harder they tried to prove God did not exist, the more they failed. One of the more current examples of this happening is of ex-atheist and author Lee Strobel. In two years of research he tried very hard to disprove God and His existence. He failed in His quest and around 1981 he accepted Jesus Christ as his personal LORD and Saviour. He has written several excellent and well-documented books that deal with the subject of God. You will not only enjoy his books, but be surprised at how much you learn from reading them. I'd recommend *The Case for Christ"* as a wonderful place to start in reading his books.

Another similar situation is how the book *"Ben Hur: A Tale of the Christ"* came to be written. Union General Lew Wallace was brought up a Christian. At some point in his life he had a conversation with Union Colonel Robert Green Ingersoll who was a well known orator and agnostic of the time. After speaking with Colonel Ingersoll, General Wallace realized that he in fact knew very little about what it means to be a Christian.

After researching the question for seven years he produced the novel *"Ben Hur"* to help bring a fuller knowledge of what it means to be a believer in Jesus Christ. His book was first published on November 12, 1880 and has never been out of print since. For many years excerpts of the great sea battle and the chariot race were included in school readers and *"Ben Hur"* remained one of the most requested books at libraries.

Scripture teaches us in Matthew 7:1-2, *"Judge not, that ye be not judged. For with what judgment ye judge, ye shall be judged: and with what measure ye mete, it shall be measured to you again."* I think it is important to stress that we not sit in judgment of any person, but possibly more so of someone who calls themselves an atheist. Unless they choose to share with you the why that they hold this belief, you can't be sure of where they are coming from. I am saying this with one person who is a dear friend in mind, but I am sure that he is not alone in his experiences with religion.

This man was by all standards of the time brought up in a very religious and Christian home. His mother, in her fear that her son might someday suffer the flames of eternal damnation, decided to give him a show and tell lesson of what hell would be like. So, she took her three year old son's hand and placed it on a hot stove burner in order that he would never be so bad that he would go to her concept of hell. He never forgot the lesson that his mother taught him that day. He never learned the true nature of God either.

To him God is not love; He is a God that justifies mothers burning little boys' hands. This is a real shame; his mother in her misguided religious zeal turned her son's heart away from God. This same man justifies his belief that God does not exist because if He did, then how can there be so much abuse of children in this world. However, if there is one, He can't be good because of all of the evil in the world.

This man has been so emotionally damaged by his mother's actions that he doesn't want to hear about man's free will choices being responsible for the evil that exists in this world. We freely choose to disobey God and follow Satan, no one twists our arms. His mind is burned shut on the God issue. What his mother did to him was pure evil; sixty plus years ago things were different, but you have to ask yourself why no one noticed this child's burned hand and did something about it. I keep him and his family in my prayers, I have full confidence that God will in some way get through to his heart, in His perfect timing.

Keep those that do not know God in your prayers and those who have been run away from God in your prayers. Ask the Holy Spirit to convict their hearts and to bring them into a personal relationship with Him. Maybe next time an atheist crosses your pathway you will remember this man and do your best to show God's mercy and love to these people. You never know the why behind their decision to not acknowledge God unless you take the time to develop a safe relationship with them. We need to show them that God is love not just try to tell them about it; how we conduct ourselves will speak louder than anything that we could ever say to them.

CHAPTER 22

HOW TO FORGIVE UNFORGIVEABLE PEOPLE

How do we go about forgiving people who have caused us so much hurt that just the idea of forgiving them seems impossible to us? Some people go to their graves holding un-forgiveness (hence sin) in their hearts. Some people even stupidly feel to hold un-forgiveness in their heart is a badge of honor. They will recite with chest thumping pride how they punished a certain person by not talking to them and the longer that they do this the more pride they take in their actions. One man I know hasn't spoken to his brother-in-law for over 20 years and still holds it as a point of honor.

Another true example (from 1952) that I personally know of is a man still holds anger in his heart and brags about how angry he still is over his younger brother wearing his brand new pair of gloves first. These examples are almost laughable, they are so ridiculous, but unfortunately they are true. Sadly, each of these men thinks that they are doing the right and honorable thing by holding onto their anger and un-forgiveness like it is a precious gemstone.

In addition to that, they feel that they are Christians in good standing with God because they are in church, in the same pew each and every week. Our Father's Words telling us that if we want forgiveness and mercy from God then we need to show the same forgiveness and mercy that we are asking for ourselves to others, just doesn't apply to them; they can't see the beam in their eyes (Matthew 7:3-5, Luke 6:41-42). Besides that, how could anyone in their right mind be even remotely inferring that they could have made a mistake or be wrong.

You and I know these people and some of us live with them and even see them in the mirror as we pass by it. Unfortunately, some of these people can be also very legalistically religious. They tend to embrace whatever the man made traditions (Mark 7:13) of their denominations are, while relegating their Bible (if they even have one) to collecting dust on the shelf. So many people will swear on the head of their beloved grandmother that they are certain something is written in the Bible while never once having opened it or even read it. Here again, my people perish for lack of knowledge (Hosea 4:6).

When we don't forgive, it turns our hearts to stone and when our hearts are turned to stone God cannot work with them. When we forgive, our hearts are like putty in God's hands. Again I do know how hard it is to forgive and especially when someone we deeply love has hurt us in what would seem in the natural to be just unforgivable. He can help us to walk through the process where we can really have a changed heart and really and truly have forgiveness in our hearts for everyone who has hurt us or wronged us in any way. We should not be able to hold on to anger in our hearts any more than we can hold water in our cupped hands. Our anger should be like that water; it should just seep out between our fingers.

Okay, so I have you sort of convinced that we need to forgive others, but how do we get to the point where we really can forgive others and truly mean it? It's not an easy process but the more that we walk it out the easier that it will become. It will still initially hurt when people offend you but God will change your heart and give you the tools that you need to be able to say I forgive them and really mean it.

The first thing that you have to do is to say to God that you forgive so and so for whatever they have done to you. You DO NOT have to mean it when you say it here because the next part of your profession of faith is that you ask God to change your heart and make this a true statement. Over time He will heal the hurt that the person has caused you to feel and He will change your heart where you are able to eventually say with a heart of love, that you do forgive that person.

Also, don't forget to ask God's forgiveness for whatever part that your actions may have played in this given situation and any other sins that you have committed. As long as we are in these flesh bodies we are going to make mistakes and as such we need to ask God's forgiveness of us each and every day. Romans 3:23 says: *"For all have sinned, and come short of the Glory of God."*

It is important here to note that you do not ever have to go to the person that has offended you and tell them that you forgive them for the hurt that they have caused you. Why? Because there are a lot of people out in the world that if you went to them and said: "I forgive you for the hurt that you have caused me by your actions" they would think you are crazy. Keep in mind that there are a lot of people who would be offended by a statement like this if it was said to them because a lot of people think that they are incapable of making a mistake. As such, they would never recognize themselves in the given situation.

The best thing that you can do in this situation like this is to take all of the hurt that this person has caused you and say to God; "I don't want this hurt in my life, I take and put all of this hurt at the foot of the cross of Jesus Christ, so that you can deal with it God." When you surrender all of the hurt that this situation has caused you to God, then God will take it and deal with it. He truly is the only one who is able to heal the hurts that our hearts will hold. We have to give it all up to Him. The traditional hymn *"I Surrender All"* is a very good song to keep in mind here and maybe even sing a bit of it. This is a good way of dealing with all the problems that you are facing, not just learning to forgive others. When we do this, He will heal the situation and our hearts.

You can also ask God to change the heart of the person who has hurt you. The best thing that we can do when we are dealing with offensive and ornery people is to give them to God. We are told in God's Holy Word to bless our enemies. Matthew 5:43-44 teaches us, *"Ye have heard that it hath been said, Thou shalt love thy neighbour, and hate thine enemy. But I say unto you, Love your enemies, bless them that curse you, do good to them that hate you, and pray for them which despitefully use you and persecute you."* Additionally, in Luke 6:27-28 scripture says: *"But I say unto you which hear, Love your enemies, do good to them which hate you, Bless them that curse you, and pray for them which despitefully use you."*

The people that seem to be able to hurt us the deepest and do the most damage to our heart are generally the ones that we love the most. So basically they are not our true enemies even though their actions may make them seem that way. Additionally their actions may make you question if these people truly love you and have your best interest at heart or in reality hate you. When we are obedient to God's Word and ask God to bless them, then God will take care of the situation for us. Scripture teaches us in Proverbs 3:3-5, *"Trust in the LORD with all thine heart; and lean not unto thine own understanding. In all thy ways acknowledge Him, and He shall direct thy paths."*

CHAPTER 23

HOW TO FORGIVE REPEAT OFFENDERS WHO HAVE NO REMORSE

Your next question may rightly be how can you forgive someone who repeatedly does the same thing to hurt you time and time again. They show absolutely no remorse for it and they seem to actually take pleasure in hurting you. Well it is hard, and you still go through all of the above steps that you have learned but you tweak it a little bit. First, you need to realize what God says on this subject. Luke 17:3-4 says, *"Take heed to yourselves: If thy brother trespass against thee, rebuke him; and if he repent, forgive him. And if he trespass against thee seven times in a day, and seven times in a day turn again to thee, saying, I repent; thou shalt forgive him."* For most of us repeatedly forgiving someone for the same offense is easier said than done, but take heart, it is not impossible with the Grace of God to do it.

My personal experience with a situation of this type concerns a person who lies most of the time. No matter how much you can prove that they are telling lies no one wants to believe the truth, the lie is so much more exciting to believe. It is very frustrating to deal with a person of this ilk. It puts you into the position of having to prove that you are the one constantly truth telling and it makes you look like you are of low character and dishonest. Now I know Our Holy Father knows the truth in this matter but it is still very hard, in the natural, to deal with it in a loving and a forgiving manner that is pleasing to God.

Scripture speaks to the subject of people who tell lies this way, *"Thy tongue deviseth mischiefs; like a sharp razor, working deceitfully. Thou lovest evil more than good; and lying rather than to speak righteousness. Selah"* (Psalm 52:2-3). Selah is used throughout scripture meaning that you should pause and really think hard upon what you have just read because of the importance of it. Psalm 120:2 continues the thoughts on the subject of lying, *"Deliver my soul, O*

LORD, *from lying lips, and from a deceitful tongue."* Again the book of Psalms speaks to the subject in chapter 31:18, *"Let the lying lips be put to silence; which speak grievous things proudly and contemptuously against the righteous."*

The book of Proverbs speaks to lying in this manner; Proverbs 6:16-19, *"These six things doth the LORD hate: yea, seven are an abomination unto Him: A proud look, a lying tongue, and hands that shed innocent blood, An heart that deviseth wicked imaginations, feet that be swift in running to mischief, A false witness that speaketh lies, and he that soweth discord among brethren."* Proverbs 12:22 continues with, *"Lying lips are abomination to the LORD: but they that deal truly are His delight."* Most dictionaries agree that an abomination is something that is detestable and justifying extreme hated or loathing of it. For God's Word to declare lying as one of the things that He calls as an abomination unto Him, means He takes the deliberate act of lying very seriously. It is a dangerous and deadly place to be if God considers your actions an abomination unto Him.

From the study of scripture the best and first concrete step that you can take is to pray on it for wisdom in how to deal with it. James 1:5 says to us, *"If any of you lack wisdom, let him ask of God, that giveth to all men liberally, and upbraideth not; and it shall be given him."* So, first we ask God for directions; and He will make it known to us how to proceed with this situation. For the most part we need to forgive said person, following all of the above mentioned steps. We "tweak" this situation by adding a couple more steps to the forgiving process.

First we mark this person in that we avoid them if at all possible. *"Now I beseech you, brethren, mark them which cause divisions and offences contrary to the doctrine which ye have learned; and avoid them. For they that are such serve not our LORD Jesus Christ, but their own belly; and by good words and fair speeches deceive the hearts of the simple"* (Romans 16:7-18). Yes, to please God we do need to forgive them but we don't have to put ourselves in a close proximity to them. If every time I took a short cut and walked through a dark alley I was mugged you can bet I would avoid that alley. Sometimes just staying away from a certain person will take care of the problem and unfortunately sometimes it doesn't. Sometimes your circumstances are made worse by the people who surround the situation. A lot of people would rather believe the worst about a person rather than have to confront a situation or a person and acknowledge the truth.

There is nothing unbiblical about avoiding someone who you know to be dishonorable and untrustworthy; and just because we are Christians doesn't mean that we have to be a door mat for anyone. In my given situation I have severed all contact with said person and I feel that if God wants to restore that relationship in my life He will make a way for it to happen. *"Now we command you, brethren, in the Name of our LORD Jesus Christ, that ye with draw yourselves from every brother that walketh disorderly, and not after the tradition which he received of us"* (2 Thessalonians 3:6).

When you are not with these problem people you take away the opportunity for them to come up with lies about you. They may still talk about you but it gets harder for them if you have no contact with them. Eventually they should lose interest in you and go on to another person who they have easier access to. God will get you past the hurt and heal your heart in these matters. You can count on it. He always takes care of His children and sometimes, God will take certain people out of your circle of friends or family for His own reasons.

We need to keep ourselves focused on the undisputable fact that Our Father God is in control of all things in our life. As His Holy Word proclaims, He will pull good out of what Satan meant for evil in our life (Genesis 50:20). I have personally found that when He pulls someone out of my life that has been important to me; He will replace them with someone better. We just have to keep our trust in Him and let Him handle the details.

CHAPTER 24

WHY SHOULD WE FORGIVE?

So again, I say to you why should we forgive? Mainly because God's Word tells us to and it pleases Him when we obey His Word. Our Father God loves obedient children no matter how old they may be. Again, don't forget that unless we show forgiveness to others God will not forgive us of our sins. A heart full of un-forgiveness and bitterness is a hardened heart and God cannot work with you if your heart is hardened. We become a vessel of dishonour to God.

Jesus Christ gives us the ultimate example of forgiveness in Luke 23:34 when He says to His Father while on the cross: *"Father, forgive them; for they know not what they do...."* If Jesus is able to forgive all of those who were responsible for crucifying Him then surely we can find it in our heart to forgive others. From the cross Jesus Christ spoke six times. *"Father, forgive them; for they know not what they do ..."* were the first words that He spoke. From this you can see the importance that God puts on forgiveness.

So, even if you have to forgive someone by (at first) just going through the motions, DO IT. Think of it as taking baby steps, we all have to start someplace. It will become easier the more that you do it, I promise. Above that, you have the satisfaction of knowing you are doing your best to be obedient to God by pleasing Him (Deuteronomy 11:26-28).

CHAPTER 25

WHAT HAVE WE LEARNED AND WHY DO WE NEED TO PRAY?

So, we have learned why we need to pray and when. We have learned how to pray including basic Spiritual Warfare tactics. We have learned about the true nature of God, and the true nature of Satan, our adversary. We have learned that God will forgive us our trespasses if we forgive others their trespasses against us. We have learned that we also need to ask God to forgive us and He will and He will help us to forgive those that we view as unforgivable to us (Matthew 6:14-15). We have learned that it is impossible to please God without faith (Hebrews 11:6). Even in all of this we still come back to the original question of why do we need to pray?

Maybe the best answer is that it pleases God when we pray to Him and it allows us to have a personal and intimate relationship with Him. Without our communicating with God we will never walk in the knowledge of our full inheritance that we have as a child of God. We again come back to Hosea 4:6, my people perish for lack of knowledge.

Scripture gives us the perfect example of how important God views prayer when we repeatedly are shown how many times Jesus Christ prayed to His Father. Here are some: St. Matthew 26:53, *"Thinkest thou that I cannot now pray to my Father, and He shall presently give me more than twelve legions of angels?"* St. John 17:9, *"I pray for them..."* Mark 14:32, *"And they came to a place which was named Gethsemane: and He saith to His disciples, Sit ye here, while I shall pray."* St. Luke 6:12, *"And it came to pass in those days, that He went out into a mountain to pray, and continued all night in prayer to God."* St. Luke 9:28, *"And it came to pass about an eight days after these sayings, He took Peter and John and James, and went up into a mountain to pray."* St. Luke 11:1, *"And it came to pass, that, as He was praying in a certain place, when He ceased, one of His disciples said unto Him, LORD, teach us to pray, as John also taught His disciples."*

CHAPTER 26

WHAT DOES GOD PROMISE TO US WHEN WE PRAY?

What does God promise to us when we pray? John 14:13-14, *"And whatsoever ye shall ask in my name, that will I do, that the Father may be glorified in the Son. If ye shall ask anything in my name, I will do it."* John 16:23-24, *"And in that day ye shall ask me nothing. Verily, verily, I say unto you, whatsoever ye shall ask the Father in my name, He will give it you. Hitherto have ye asked nothing in my name: ask, and ye shall receive, that your joy may be full."*

Additional Holy Scriptures are: Matthew 6:5-7, *"And when thou prayest, thou shalt not be as the hypocrites are: for they love to pray standing in the synagogues and in the corners of the streets, that they may be seen of men. Verily I say unto you, they have their reward. But thou, when thou prayest, enter into thy closet, and when thou hast shut thy door, pray to thy Father which is in secret; and thy Father which seeth in secret shall reward thee openly. But when ye pray, use not vain repetitions, as the heathen do: for they think that they shall be heard for their much speaking."* Luke 11:9-10, *"And I say unto you, Ask, and it shall be given you; seek, and ye shall find; knock, and it shall be opened unto you. For every one that asketh receiveth; and he that seeketh findeth; and to him that knocketh it shall be opened."*

CHAPTER 27

WHEN AND HOW WILL GOD ANSWER OUR PRAYERS?

God will answer our prayers in His perfect timing. Will God answer all of our prayers? Yes, one way or another all of our prayers are answered. God will answer our prayers according to His perfect Will and Way for us. If you pray to God to be the best bank robber in the world I would not expect that to happen. But if you pray to be the best in your class, or the best at your job those petitions are in the Will of God for you. These do not go against His commandments.

Proverbs 4:20-22, teaches us, *"My son, attend to my words; incline thine ear unto my saying. Let them not depart from thine eyes; keep them in the midst of thine heart. For they are life unto those that find then, and health to all their flesh."* It is important that you know that when you decide to start praying and having a deeper relationship with God that you are not going to make the devil happy. He will repeatedly try to attack you spiritually to stop you dead in your tracks and make you question your decision to have a relationship with God.

Satan does not bother attacking what he already controls, so be aware that he will attack you and if he can't get to you he will come at you through what and who you love most. That is why we discussed Spiritual Warfare and the tools that God has given us to deal with Satan and have victory over him. Remember here that Satan is a defeated foe.

1st Peter 3:18-22 verifies it: *"For Christ also hath once suffered for sins, the just for the unjust, that He might bring us to God, being put to death in the flesh, but quickened by the Spirit: By which also He went and preached unto the spirits in prison; Which sometime were disobedient, when once the longsuffering* (meaning patience) *of God waited in the days of Noah, while the ark was a preparing, wherein few, that is eight souls were saved by water. The like figure whereunto even baptism doth also now save us (not the putting away of the filth of the flesh, but the answer of a good conscience toward God,) by the resurrection of Jesus Christ; Who is gone into heaven, and is on the right hand of God; angels and authorities and powers being make subject unto Him."* Christ's Blood on the cross gave us the victory that we have over Satan. No doubt about it, Satan is a defeated foe.

How does God answer our prayers? God will answer our prayers in His perfect Will and His perfect timing. 1st John 5:14, states, *"And this is the confidence that we have in Him, that, if we ask any thing according to His Will, He heareth us: And if we know that He hear us, whatsoever we ask, we know that we have the petitions that we desired of Him."* 1st John 3:22, further says, *"And whatsoever we ask, we receive of Him, because we keep His commandments, and do those things that are pleasing in His sight."*

Sometimes we have an almost instant answer. Other times it may take years. Remember when it does take longer than what we would like it to, it is a process and the length of time that it takes is so that we can learn from this situation. The book of James tells us in all things count it joy because God will work this out for His Glory and your benefit. We have lessons to learn in this life time, and waiting patiently for God to answer our prayers is an important one to learn.

Psalm 46:10 says to us, *"Be still, and know that I am God..."* Isaiah 40:31 teaches us: *"But they that wait upon the LORD shall renew their strength; they shall mount up with wings as eagles; they shall run, and not be weary; and they shall walk, and not faint."* Isaiah 30:18 teaches us: *"And therefore will the LORD wait, that He may be gracious unto you, and therefore will He be exalted, that He may have mercy upon you: for the LORD is a God of judgment: blessed are all they that wait for Him."*

CHAPTER 28

WHY DOES IT SEEM THAT THE WICKED PROSPER?

Another question that a lot of people want answered is why does it seem that the wicked people of this world prosper? You will find the answer to that is Psalm 37. Here are the main parts that answer the question. Psalm 37:7-9, *"Rest in the LORD, and wait patiently for Him: fret not thyself because of him who prospereth in his way, because of the man who bringeth wicked devices to pass. Cease from anger, and forsake wrath: fret not thyself in any wise to do evil. For evildoers shall be cut off: but those that wait upon the LORD, they shall inherit the earth."* Psalm 37:20, *"But the wicked shall perish, and the enemies of the LORD shall be as the fat of lambs: they shall consume; into smoke shall they consume away."* Psalm 47:34, *"Wait on the LORD, and keep His way, and He shall exalt thee to inherit the land; when the wicked are cut off, thou shalt see it."*

This translates into don't ever think that the wicked prosper, for they will be as the fat that drips onto an open fire and goes up in smoke and just disappears into the air. You are going to be blessed in that God will let you see the wicked corrected. Romans 12:19-21 further teaches us; *"Dearly beloved, avenge not yourselves, but rather give place unto wrath (*set it aside*); for it is written, Vengeance is mine; I will repay, saith the LORD. Therefore if thine enemy hunger, feed him; if he thirst, give him drink; for in so doing thou shalt heap coals of fire* (shame) *on his head. Be not overcome of evil but overcome evil with good."*

CHAPTER 29

HOW DO WE GO ABOUT PRAYING TO GOD?

So how do we go about praying to God? A good place to start is with "The Our Father" from Matthew 6:9-13. This is the perfect example that Jesus gave to the disciples when asked how they should pray.

THE OUR FATHER

Our Father which art in heaven,
Hallowed be thy name
Thy Kingdom come,
Thy Will be done in earth,
As it is in heaven
Give us this day our daily bread
And forgive us our debts,
As we forgive our debtors
And lead us not into temptation,
But deliver us from evil:
For thine is the Kingdom,
And the power,
And the glory,
For ever,
Amen.

How else can we pray? The 23rd Psalm is a very reassuring and calming Psalm to pray. To have a deeper understanding of the 23rd Psalm Max Lucado's book *"Safe in the Shepherd's Arms"* is an excellent place to learn.

PSALM 23

The LORD is my shepherd;
I shall not want.

He maketh me to lie down in green pastures:
He leadeth me beside the still waters.
He restoreth my soul:
He leadeth me in the paths
Of righteousness
For His name's sake

Yea, though I walk
Through the valley
Of the Shadow of Death,
I will fear no evil:
For thou art with me;
Thy rod and thy staff
They comfort me.

Thou preparest a table
Before me
In the presence
Of mine enemies;
Thou anointest
My head with oil;
My cup runneth over.

Surely goodness
And mercy
Shall follow me
All the days of my life:
And I will dwell
In the house
Of the LORD
Forever

Psalm 91 is another excellent Psalm to pray with. It is a Psalm of protection.

PSALM 91

*He that dwelleth
In the secret place
Of the Most High
Shall abide
Under the Shadow* of the Almighty*

*I will say of the LORD,
He is my refuge
And my fortress:
My God;
In Him will I trust*

*Surely He shall deliver thee
From the snare of the fowler,
And from the noisome pestilence***

*He shall cover thee
With His feathers,
And under His wings
Shalt thou trust,
His truth
Shall be thy shield
And buckler.*

*Thou shalt not
Be afraid
For the terror by night;
Nor for the arrow
That flieth by day;*

*Shadow, meaning: "defense".
**Pestilence, meaning: "evil plague".

*Nor for the pestilence
That walketh in darkness;
Nor for the destruction
That wasteth at noonday.*

*A thousand
Shall fall at thy side,
And ten thousand
At thy right hand;
But it shall not come nigh thee.*

*Only with thine eyes
Shalt thou behold
And see the reward
Of the wicked*

*Because
Thou hast made the LORD,
Which is my refuge
Even the Most High,
Thy habitation;*

*There shall no evil befall thee,
Neither shall any plague
Come nigh thy dwelling.*

*For He shall give
His angels
Charge over thee,
To keep thee
In all thy ways*

*They shall bear thee up
In their hands,
Lest thou dash thy foot
Against a stone*

*Thou shalt
Tread upon the lion and adder;
The young lion
And the dragon
Shalt thou trample under feet

Because
He has set His love upon me,

Therefore
Will I deliver Him:

I will set Him on high,
Because He hath known my name

He shall call upon me,
And I will answer Him:

I will be with Him in trouble;

I will deliver Him,
And honour Him.

With long life
Will I satisfy Him,
And show him my salvation.*

CHAPTER 30

PRAYING OVER SERIOUS SITUATIONS IN YOUR LIFE

The next three Psalms are excellent to pray when you are dealing with a serious situation in your life. There are many more than these three but these are just to give you an example of how to use scripture to pray on your problems. Sometimes our problems are just small bumps in our pathway to navigate around and other times we have a whole mountain range of problems to overcome.

When you find yourself in a crisis time I highly suggest that you purchase a notebook to write down scriptures (verses) you find appropriate to the issues that you are dealing with. Use this note book everyday to pray from. Keep adding scripture to it as you dig deeper into God's Word to help you learn and grow from this. You will be surprised at how many scriptures you will find that speak personally to you about your problems. The more you are in God's Word the more that He will reveal to you. If you fill up your notebook with scripture then get a second notebook and start filling that one too.

All of this time you will be growing in your personal relationship with God and God will bring peace to your heart and mind and good will eventually come out of the problem that you are wrestling with (Genesis 50:20). Do not forget to praise and thank God for what you are going through. Remember that you are in a smelting fire and the finished product will be more beautiful than you can even imagine.

Philippians 4:4-7, *"Rejoice in the LORD always: and again I say, rejoice. Let your moderation be known unto all men. The LORD is at hand. Be careful for nothing* (meaning: don't be anxious about anything)*; but in everything by prayer and supplication with thanksgiving let your requests be made known unto God. And the peace of God, which passeth all understanding, shall keep your hearts and* *minds though Christ Jesus."* Additionally Philippians 4:13 teaches us, *"I can do all things through Christ which strengtheneth me."*

PSALM 5

*Give ear to my words, O LORD,
Consider my meditation.*

*Hearken unto the voice of my cry,
My King, and my God;
For unto thee will I pray.*

*My voice shalt thou hear
In the morning,
O LORD;*

*In the morning
Will I direct
My prayer unto thee,
And will look up.*

*For thou art not a God
That hath pleasure in wickedness:*

*Neither shall evil
Dwell with thee.*

*The foolish
Shall not stand in thy sight:*

*Thou hatest
All workers of iniquity*

*Thou shall
Destroy them
That speak leasing**

*The LORD will abhor
The bloody** and deceitful man.*

*But as for me,
I will come into thy house*

*And in thy fear
Will I worship towards thy holy temple.*

*Lead me, O LORD,
In thy righteousness*

*Because of mine enemies;
Make thy way straight before my face.*

*For there is no faithfulness in their mouth;
Their inward part is very wickedness;*

*Their throat is an open sepulcher***;
They flatter with their tongue.*

Destroy thou them, O God;

*Let them fall
By their own counsels;*

*Cast them out
In the multitude of their transgressions;
For they have rebelled against thee.*

*Leasing means "to lie".
**Bloody refers to someone who draws blood which causes death in man or animal.
***Sepulcher means "grave".

*But let all those
That put their trust in thee rejoice:*

*Let them ever shout for joy,
Because thou defendest them:*

*Let them
Also that love thy name
Be joyful in thee.*

For thou, LORD,

*Wilt bless the righteous;
With favour*

*Wilt thou compass him
As with a shield.*

PSALM 56

Be merciful unto me, O God:

*For man would swallow me up;
He fighting daily oppresseth me.*

*Mine enemies
Would daily swallow me up:*

*For they be many
That fight against me,
O thou Most High*

*What time I am afraid,
I will trust in thee.*

In God I will praise His Word,
In God I have put my trust;
I will not fear what flesh can do unto me.

Every day they wrest my words:
All their thoughts are against me for evil.

They gather themselves together,
They hide themselves,
They mark my steps,
When they wait for my soul.

Shall they escape by iniquity?
In thine anger cast down they people, O God

Thou tellest my wandering:
Put thou my tears into thy bottle:
Are they not in thy book?

When I cry unto thee,
Then shall mine enemies turn back:
This I know; for God is for me

In God will I praise His Word:
In the LORD will I praise His Word.

In God have I put my trust:
I will not be afraid what man can do unto me.

Thy vows are upon me,
O God:
I will render praises unto thee.

For thou hast delivered my soul from death:
Wilt not thou deliver my feet from falling,
That I may walk before God in the light of the living?

PSALM 57

Be merciful unto me, O God,
Be merciful unto me:

For my soul trusteth in thee:

Yea, in the shadow of thy wings will I make my refuge,
Until these calamities be overpast.

I will cry unto God Most High;
Unto God that performeth all things for me.

He shall send from heaven,
And save me from the reproach
Of him that would swallow me up.

Selah.

God shall send forth His mercy and His truth.

My soul is among lions:
And I lie even among them that are set on fire,

Even the sons of men,
Whose teeth are spears and arrows,
And their tongue a sharp sword.

Be thou exalted,
O God,

Above the heavens;
Let thy glory be above all the earth.

They have prepared a net for my steps;
My soul is bowed down:

They have digged a pit before me,
Into the midst
Whereof they are fallen themselves

Selah.

My heart is fixed, O God,
My heart is fixed:
I will sing and give praise.

Awake up, my glory;
Awake, psaltery and harp:
I myself will awake early.

I will praise thee,
O LORD,

Among the people:
I will sing unto thee among the nations.

For thy mercy is great unto the heavens,
And thy truth unto the clouds.

Be thou exalted,
O God,

Above the heavens:
Let thy glory be above all the earth.

CHAPTER 31

WHAT DOES SCRIPTURE SAY ABOUT CHILDREN?

Genesis 1:26-28, *"And God said, Let us make man in our image, after our likeness: and let them have dominion over the fish of the sea, and over the fowl of the air, and over the cattle, and over all the earth, and over every creeping thing that creepeth upon the earth. So God created man in His own image, in the image of God created He him; male and female created He them. And God blessed them, and God said unto them, Be fruitful, and multiply, and replenish the earth, and subdue it; and have dominion over the fish of the sea, and over the fowl of the air, and over every living thing that moveth upon the earth."* Psalm 127:3 further demonstrates for us that God holds children to be a blessing to a man and a woman, *"Lo, children are an heritage of the LORD and the fruit of the womb is His reward."*

The family is the backbone of our society. The family structure provides order to our society. Any opportunity that Satan has to wreak havoc in a marriage and a family he will wholeheartedly take it and it will provide him and his demons with much pleasure. Without intact families we have chaos which can result in young people joining gangs to find a perverted form of structure in their lives or acting out in socially unacceptable ways. We have young men growing up without a proper model of what the role of the husband and father is in the home. On our television and movie screens the role of men and fathers is constantly ridiculed and denigrated. Men are portrayed as being stupid and not worthy of any being given respect. Women are glorified for their bodies and how many different men they have slept with. Traditional values such as modesty and chastity are viewed as being archaic.

Our culture today pressures our young people to rid themselves of the oppressive burden of their virginity as soon as possible. Having sex is viewed as no big deal, possibly of no more importance than a bee going from flower to flower to pollinate it. Sexually Transmitted Diseases are the norm for our young people, not the exception. We have young women growing up thinking that the only value that they have is in their sexuality and repeatedly looking for a father figure with each man that they try to please. Without the covering that a Biblically structured family provides, our children cannot stretch and grow up in a safe and secure environment that allows them to discover who they are in Christ and what and where their true talents and gifts are.

Children reared in a loving home with a mom that shows respect and love to her husband and a father that shows love and respect to his wife (Ephesians 5:33) are able to thrive and to see Biblical love and headship in action. Biblical headship does not mean that the man lords over the woman. Think of Biblical headship as a large oak tree; the canopy or the covering branches would be the role that a man provides in the home and family structure. Like a large umbrella, he protects the family, and he is the first line of defense between the elements and his precious wife and children. He is their shield and fortress that protects them.

The woman is the tree trunk that is solidly rooted; she is the anchor for this family. She nurtures the family and the relationships within the family. Biblical headship is not about women being slaves to men. In a true Biblical headship relationship the man loves his wife more than he loves his own life, he puts her first in all things (Ephesians 5:28). He is the person who ultimately has the responsibility for the family (Genesis 3:9) but the decisions that he makes for the family are made after carefully considering the input from his wife and showing respect to her opinions. This is how God designed the family to function, the world has perverted it.

The current culture seems to view men as just sperm donors and wallets. A stay at home mom is as archaic a term as a buggy whip; both were considered useful and necessary in the past but both items are rarely seen in our current culture. Impersonal day cares have replaced moms because our current society says that anyone can nurture our children. The God given role of mother and father is viewed as interchangeable with whomever is readily available and usually that is someone to whom your child is seen as a part of their job; just one more chin to wipe and diaper to change. When parents value money over their children's welfare they are allowing other people to impart their values and morals or possibly even the government's version of morals and values into their child. Our society wants instant gratification but is it possible to survive and even live well without all of the newest gadgets? A resounding yes to the asked question; this is part of having your priorities in order.

If you truly feel that you can't survive without certain creature comforts then put off having a family until you can afford it. Unfortunately, today many children come into families that see them as accessories rather than a blessing. Instead of things being worked around the baby and the baby's needs, the baby is somehow forced to fit into the regular schedule. Don't buy into the lie that the world promotes that day care centers are okay, nothing can replace a loving mother in the home, rearing children in a Godly fashion.

In the early 1970's there was a popular song written by Sandy and Harry Chapin called *"Cat's in the Cradle"*. If you are not familiar with it, the lyrics can easily be found on the internet and probably also the song. Listen to it. Children are a blessing to a family, they are not an inconvenience. A mother in the home has one of the most important jobs in the whole world. She is shaping the next generation of young people.

If you take the time to do any sort of work with children or even teenagers you can tell the ones that have been blessed by having a loving mother in the home and Biblical discipline too; you can also tell the ones that have been brought up in a day care; they stand out like a sore thumb. There is wisdom in the old saying "that the hand that rocks the cradle rules the world" and there is even a poem by that title by William Ross Wallace. Our children deserve our very best, not just crumbs from leftovers. So much of the apathy, lack of respect in all areas, and emotional disconnecting that we see in our young people today is born out of neglect of our precious children.

CHAPTER 32

HOW TO PRAY FOR BADLY BEHAVING SPOUSES (YOU'RE NOT WITHOUT HOPE)

How should we pray when a spouse is behaving badly and possibly even thinking of walking away from the marriage? Any time there is strife in your marriage Satan is feasting on it and celebrating. God ordained the institution of marriage in Genesis 2:18, *"And the LORD God said it is not good that the man should be alone; I will make him an help meet for him."* Genesis 2:21-24, *"And the LORD God caused a deep sleep to fall upon Adam, and he slept: and He took one of his ribs, and closed up the flesh instead thereof; And the rib, which the LORD God had taken from man, made He a woman, and brought her unto the man. And Adam said this is now bone of my bones, and flesh of my flesh: she shall be called Woman, because she was taken out of Man. Therefore shall a man leave his father and his mother, and shall cleave unto his wife: and they shall be one flesh."*

You've no doubt heard the key phrase in regards to realty; location, location, location. Well in marriage the key phrase could easily be said to be communication, communication, communication. When you first were dating your spouse, you may have felt the sun and the moon revolved around them. Like most of us you fell madly in love and felt you could not live without this person by your side.

You got engaged, married, and as time went on probably had a couple of kids along the way. Sometimes we get so busy just in trying to do everything that parents are required to do in a 24 hour period that the "we" part of us continually gets pushed to the side and almost becomes nonexistent. One of the things that you have to acknowledge here is if you are in this situation then your priorities are out of order.

We have to go back to basics: acknowledge God first in all things (*"But seek ye first the kingdom of God, and His righteousness..."* Matthew

6:33), spouse second, children third, and the rest of the world can get in line and take a number. Here too, be extremely cautious with the amount of time that you spend talking on the phone when your spouse is with you. If you have to be on the phone, by all means do so but keep it as short as possible. When you take time away from what the two of you should be doing then you are showing disrespect to your spouse. This applies to any time that you spend that you are doing something that does not include your spouse.

You got married because you loved this person more than anyone else in the world and couldn't see yourself living your life without them in it. You wanted to spend all or most of your time with this person. A root of some of the problems that can arise in a marriage stems from not doing things as a couple and not showing respect to the time that you have together as a couple. We take it for granted that our spouse won't mind if we put other activities in front of our time as a couple and this is wrong thinking.

God has blessed your marriage and it is not His intention that you divorce but with that said there are rare exceptions to this rule; if your spouse is physically abusing you, if there has been infidelity, incest, and/or homosexuality for instance. These are all sins that can be forgiven by the spouse but it takes quite a bit of work to get to the point where you can rebuild trust again and really feel safe and secure in your relationship.

Do not despair, these are Biblically fixable things. The only limitation that our God has is the limits that our lack of faith put upon Him. You tie His hands from working in your life when you doubt He can or would help you. God is able to restore and renew the worst broken marriage even where the sense of betrayal and abandonment is so totally overwhelming. When you are in the mist of so much emotional pain that you find it's just hard to think clearly, God, in His ultimate mercy and grace for you, will still give you reason to smile through the veil of your tears.

God is quite capable of seamlessly re-knitting a marriage's relationship no matter how badly it has been damaged. Luke 1:37 says, *"For with God nothing shall be impossible."* Joel 2:25 speaks to us with, *"And I will restore to you the years that the locust hath eaten, the cankerworm, and the caterpillar, and the palmerworm..."* Next to the death of a child or a spouse I can't imagine going through anything worse than having your spouse say to you that they have found someone new, that they really love, that they know now that they never really loved you, and that they want a divorce so that they can go marry someone else who really understands them.

Additionally, that is the person they want standing by their side when your children get married too! Besides that, you're still young enough and attractive enough that it won't be too long before you find someone new yourself to replace them. Besides all of that, they are positive that God brought this new person into their life because they prayed for God to fix the marriage and presto, a new, more exciting person comes in front of them, so it must be God's Will and with His blessings too!

Unless you have personally experienced someone saying these words or similar words to you it is impossible to fully understand how you would react in a situation like this. I think we have all at one time or another jokingly said to our spouses that if we ever caught them cutting out on us, that we would most likely kill them and hang their hide on the garage wall or something to that effect. We may not have said this nicely but the intent of our statement was understood very clearly by our spouse.

Your first reaction may be disbelief as to the words that you are hearing coming out of your spouse's mouth. How could someone that you have spent the majority of your life with, raised children with, and love with your whole heart really think that you would have no problem in giving them a divorce. Physically, your heart goes into a kind of shock. Your heart actually hurts. You can't eat or sleep, you just walk around numb and crying tears of hurt and disbelief.

This is a nasty, nasty time in your life. But even as bad as this situation is we still have to forgive and give all of our immense hurt over to God. I know that it takes time to get to that place but if you hold all of these negative emotions inside of yourself they will eat you alive and turn you into a bitter and hateful person.

We have all seen or personally know divorced people who years after they have divorced their spouse, act and speak as if all of the nastiness from their divorce happened yesterday. They are still trying to get even with their ex-spouse. This is not God's Will to simmer with goals of revenge in our heart for our ex-spouse. We forgive because God's Word tells us to but we also forgive because God can't heal our heart unless we forgive those who have hurt us first.

I am the last person who would tell you to give up on your marriage no matter what your spouse has done. It is possible to resuscitate a marriage that most people would feel is all but dead and buried. God is the expert at resurrecting what most people view as dead and it is just a matter of turning it over to Him. This is one of those crisis moments in our lives when we are so very hurt, desperate and desolate that we get down on our knees and cry our heart out to God truly realizing maybe for the first time in our lives that God is the only person who is able to fix something this big and this bad.

I know to some people that my thinking here is being totally unrealistic but my God is a great big God and NOTHING is impossible with Him and His Word does not come back void, it comes back for His purpose and pleasure. Isaiah 55:8-11 clearly confirms this, *"For my thoughts are not your thoughts, neither are your ways my ways, saith the LORD. For as the heavens are higher than the earth, so are my ways higher than your ways, and my thoughts than your thoughts. For as the rain cometh down, and the snow from heaven, and returneth not thither, but watereth the earth, and maketh it bring forth and bud, that it may give seed to the sower, and bread to the eater: So shall my Word be that goeth forth out of my mouth: it shall not return unto me void, but it shall accomplish that which I please and it shall prosper in the thing whereto I send it."*

It is possible to restore a marriage that has been shattered, it will take a strong commitment to God and digging religiously into His Word and letting His Word heal your marriage. This is possible even when your spouse has run away from home and all responsibilities associated with home and family. Additionally this is possible even when your spouse has embraced a new, younger and improved version of you and has moved in with them. I did not say that this would be easy but it can be done, Philippians 4:13 declares, *"I can do all things through Christ which strengtheneth me."*

CHAPTER 33

HOW TO START RESTORING YOUR MARRIAGE?

I guess the best place to start in healing your marriage is to pray to God to make a way to restore it. Of course, this would be after you have asked God to help you forgive BOTH your spouse and (this next one may be even harder) the other person involved with your spouse. This all takes time. It is not an overnight thing. You need to ask forgiveness of God for whatever your part in this situation has been. Problems of this magnitude just don't develop over night; there were probably all sorts of signs that were obvious that you just missed. Most times there are signs and our minds just don't go there because it's not on our radar because it is such an unthinkable thought to us.

Every day, by digging into His Word, you will find the peace that passes understanding in His Word and by searching His Word you will develop an intimate relationship with our Father. Ask those that care and love you to pray for your spouse that the Holy Spirit will convict their heart and bring them into a full repentance so that your marriage can be healed. Not everyone is going to be on the same page as you are in this. A lot of people will expect you to speak horrible things against your spouse and they will want blood, not prayers. Additionally a lot of people will not understand the importance of praying in a situation like this. How you conduct yourself throughout this trial will reflect your faith walk with God.

You may find people will ask you how can you forgive and still love someone who has caused you so much hurt and pain. The best way to answer that question is to smile at them and truthfully say it is only by the grace and mercy of our Father God. It is not unusual for this statement to be met with silence and a weird look that gives the impression that you have gone over and around the bend (maybe even several bends).

Keep in mind here that our God is our Jehovah-Jireh; He is able and willing to provide for all of our needs. When your marriage is healed and re-blessed by God, these same people may reject your repentant spouse *and* you. This is where you will find out who your true friends and family are. If they truly love you, they will accept and be pleased that God has healed your marriage. If they don't, then they may always keep you at arm's length because somehow, in their mind, you are just not good enough for them now. You and your spouse are damaged goods.

Remember here too, some people take the attitude that once a person cheats that they will always be a cheater. They don't leave room for God being able to change a person's heart and attitudes. Possibly these might be some of the type people that feel it is okay to hold grudges and all that forgiveness stuff just doesn't apply here. With this type of situation I tend to take the attitude that if Jesus Christ can find time to forgive everyone responsible for crucifying Him then why can't they forgive someone else especially since anything that we can do in this flesh body is nowhere as grievous as crucifying Christ.

Keep positive professions of faith over your spouse; pray them every day. It is an excellent idea to also see a Christian Counselor to help you deal with all of the emotions that you are going through. They will give you additional tools to help you go through this trial and keep your sanity. When you look for a Christian Counselor it is important to find one who is trained in Christian counseling. Many people think that being a Christian counselor just means that the person believes in God; and that would be a wrong answer.

A true Christian Counselor is a counselor who has been trained in counseling that has God at the center of it. There is a world of difference between a true Christian Counselor and a secular counselor. The one will be positive because they are looking at what God can do and what God's Word says on the subject, the other is looking at what the secular world says and their attitude is very likely to be what are you going to do with yourself after your divorce comes through. They are very negative; it may take you a little bit of elbow grease but seek out a Christian Counselor and stick with a Christian Counselor only. They are worth their weight in gold.

CHAPTER 34

LIFE CHANGES IN MEN AND WOMEN

There are a lot of changes that happen to us in life and a lot of them are directly related to how we are aging. Women go through Menopause and that in itself is quite an adjustment because it really throws your hormones out of balance and that creates chaos in all areas of our lives. The Law of Gravity leaves an imprint upon all of our bodies too; and if it's not Menopause or gravity, then it's the ten or twelve years prior to Menopause called Perimenopause that affects your body in negative ways also. Most people don't even think or acknowledge that it can have impact upon your marriage because it adds to the stress on your hormones. So for most females you may realize that you are stressed out or just don't feel right but you don't understand the source of it; it's like being blindsided by your own body.

Of course there is the stigma of Menopause because when you are officially defined as a Menopausal female it's the one milestone in your life that our culture says certifies you as being "old, worn out and useless." Now I don't believe this but a lot of people do. You just have to watch current T.V. ads to see that our culture places a high value on youth and being youthful. If you're over fifty the commercials have you most likely worried about incontinence, constipation, and dentures.

Men go through their own form of Menopause but it is called Andropause. It is usually accompanied by a decrease in their level of testosterone which in turn is responsible for changes in their attitudes and moods, fatigue, loss of energy and sex drive, and a loss of physical agility. So most likely they get grumpy and gain weight.

Some anti-aging doctors call this "Grumpy Old Men Syndrome" because they become grumpy old men and they are not always pleasant to be with and sometimes even downright ornery; they are just not happy people anymore. A lower testosterone level also equals weaker bones for men and an increase in heart disease and diabetes. All of this can add up to what is commonly called a Mid-life Crisis and yes, there are additional reasons for men to have a Mid-life Crisis too!

Men especially tie their worth and definition to their jobs, and somewhere around 40 to 60ish they start to question their values, their accomplishments in life, and the direction of their lives. They seem to be asking themselves the question "Is that all there is?" So what has been comfortable to them all of a sudden they are desperate to change it. At this point a lot of them really act stupid and they will even put at risk everything including their wife, children, health and job that they have valued in their life.

It's like they are sitting on a hot seat. They are so antsy; nothing seems to make them happy so they start looking outside their comfortable lives to find happiness. Sometimes this might be the middle aged man who comes home with the fancy red sports car that he really thinks makes him more sexually attractive and youthful, in spite of the fact that he may throw his back out just trying to get into it. Sometimes men feel the only way that they can find true happiness is to trade in the old wife. This is really sad. Ecclesiastes 9:9 teaches us, *"Live joyfully with the wife whom thou lovest all the days of the life of thy vanity, which He hath given thee under the sun, all the days of thy vanity: for that is thy portion in this life, and in thy labour which thou takest under the sun."*

In regards to Menopause and Andropause we can't stop our bodies from aging but we don't have to go down without a fight to keep our bodies as youthful and healthy as possible. Maybe part of our marriage vows should be that we vow to exercise and eat right and to encourage our spouses to do so also. When you get married the last thing on your mind is crows' feet and stretch marks and of course other people will get fat but not you. When you are first married the odds are your body and your metabolism are working well for you both and you can pretty much eat and physically do whatever you want to. Knees that don't bend well and stiff joints and backs will never happen to you; that's for old people.

Life is about change and dealing gracefully with the changes in our physical body is part of the "for better or worse" of your vows.

You can't blame every problem on weight gain or injuries, but if you both work on staying healthy together it makes the battle easier. If one of you is injured and not able to do everything physically that you could before don't be afraid to try something as simple but very effective as seeking out a physical therapist.

You don't have to accept the status quo after an injury; unfortunately a lot of our doctors would rather hand you a jar of pain pills or give you an injection than actually bother with aiming you toward a physical therapist or some other person who could actually help to restore you to good health. A lot of our health problems that we accumulate as we grow older are directly related to our life style and our food habits. God designed our bodies with the ability to heal, but that won't happen unless we feed it properly and exercise it well. We need to exercise responsible stewardship with our bodies and health.

If you need help in finding a good doctor to help you age gracefully; I suggest that you look for a doctor whose specialty is anti-aging. This type of doctor will balance out both husband and wife's hormones. You may not have heard of this type of doctor but they have been around since the early 1990's. Back in the early 1960's allergists were relatively new to the medical specialty field and now everyone is aware of what they do and they are totally accepted by the medical community.

Well anti-aging doctors are just now starting to be more common but they do not have the full acceptance of the medical community yet. There are a lot of doctors that do not feel that the study of anti-aging is a valid field of medical science; they seem to think that if we are over 50 we should just silently accept the fact that we are older and not expect too much of yourself. Anti-aging doctors hold the theory that we don't age because we get older, but we age because our hormones decline.

These anti-aging doctors validate that life over fifty can have a rich vitality to it and their passion is to help us live our life to its fullest. They don't discount you just because you're old enough to get free coffee at some restaurants. This is a good place to start in keeping yourself healthy as you age and will also benefit your marriage. Plus, this is one doctor that you can both see.

This is not the same as artificial hormone replacement therapy (HRT) because you are not dealing with the manmade chemicals; anti-aging doctors only use bioidenticals which mean that they come from God given sources in nature. You most likely have heard negative comments from drug companies about them, but keep in mind that because the drug companies can't make money off of a natural ingredient they are not going to be supportive of a product that does not increase their purse. Check it out, and make up your own mind on the subject; only you can decide if it will benefit you or not.

CHAPTER 35

WHERE DOES GOOD NUTRITION FIT INTO A MARRIAGE?

While we are on the subject, God has given us everything that we need to stay healthy. If you look at the examples of all of the times that God fed people in the Bible, you will see that He fed them with simple foods not chemically designed foods. Food manufacturers can't make much money off of simple foods; if they add things to them then they can charge you more for them. So much of the food that is sold as nutritious in our grocery stores is really just empty calories and high carbohydrates. Unfortunately, often times the boxes that the so called food comes in will have a higher nutritional value than what's in the box.

Take flour for example: wheat in its natural state has nearly thirty vitamins and minerals in it. God made it a near perfect food. Once it is processed to be sold as white flour, all of the vitamins and minerals are stripped out of it. When we buy wheat as white flour in the grocery store the label tells us it is enriched because the food manufacturer's have graciously added back a few of the cheaper B vitamins that it originally had before being stripped out of it. If you want to get the rest of the vitamins and minerals that it originally came with you can buy a jar of wheat germ for about five bucks.

Now if you buy 100% whole wheat flour it should have everything that God made it with, in it. The problem is that most people don't buy whole wheat flour for their cooking and baking needs. All purpose, enriched and bleached white flour is the flour of choice for most American homes. There is a saying in nutritional circles that says the whiter the bread, the quicker you're dead. White bread is extremely popular in these United States.

An example of how the food manufacturers have tinkered with our food products is that for a while you would find brominated flour in our bread products and even our flour that you could buy. The manufacturers added this to the flour because it made the bread more elastic and the dough stronger. Sounds good, like a win-win situation doesn't it, except that after a while people found out that bromating flour possibly led to cancer. The theory was that all of the cancer causing agents would bake out of the product but unfortunately a little of it was left over and that in itself was worrisome to the health experts. So now, for the most part brominated flour is considered illegal.

We have a God given responsibility to take care of these temples that God has given us (1st Corinthians 3:16-17). Learn how to read labels for your health. It's like that old saying "garbage in, garbage out" and it just doesn't apply to what we eat. If all you take in through your eyes and ears is trash, i.e., soap operas, trashy shows that ridicule traditional values, shows that every other word is just filth, shows that glorify sex outside of marriage, and on and on it goes. You get the picture. The more you expose yourself to this trash, the more common it becomes to you and eventually it just becomes no big deal. You become desensitized to it all and every time that you view these types of programs they will erode your Christian values just a little bit more.

To get back to God feeding people in the Bible, take the time Jesus fed the 5000 men, plus women and children in Matthew chapter 14, Luke chapter 9, Mark chapter 6 and John chapter 6. He fed them with two small fishes and five small loafs of Barley Bread. Barley Bread was considered bread that the poor people would most likely be eating and also it was considered animal feed. So the bread that Jesus fed this group was very basic, certainly not a meal fit for a King in the traditional sense.

Let's take a closer look at that Barley Bread. Barley is one of those grains that are nutritionally superb like wheat. So, even though it was not a "fancy meal", nutrition wise it had everything in it to keep people healthy. Today people pay a premium at health food stores to buy "greens". Greens have barley grasses in them and they are considered by many to be nutritionally superior to most foods that you would find in a normal grocery store. Do some research on the subject and take time to educate yourself as to what is good nutrition. Our bodies do come with an owner's manual; it is called The Holy Bible. God has given us perfect foods to eat, we just have to rediscover them and reacquaint our palates with them.

The Bible is our source for all of the answers to all of our questions. We just need to be smart enough to figure that out. This is all part of taking good care of yourself, and your family. In case you don't know where to start let me suggest several excellent sources from people who are both well educated on nutrition and also are men and women of God.

Dr. Jordan S. Rubin is the author of *"The Makers Diet"* and additional books; Dr. Bob Demaria has written *"Dr. Bob's Transfat Survival Guide"* and additional books; Dr. Don Colbert and his wife Mary have written *"The Seven Pillars of Health"* and additional books; and Dr. Ted Broer and his wife Sharon have written over ten books on how to obtain good health Biblically. Dr. Valerie Saxion is another excellent source to learn about good nutrition from and how it impacts your health. She has written many books on nutrition and health issues and even has a cable T.V. program called "Alternative Health" which you can find on Trinity Broadcasting Network. In fact, The Trinity Broadcasting Network will often feature all of the above named doctors on their many fine programs.

Any of these Biblically centered doctors will provide good and safe information as to how to reclaim your health no matter how high the mileage is on your body and how much tread you have lost. These books are an excellent source of information on keeping and maintaining good health no matter how young or old you are. This information will bless all members of your family.

One additional lesson to learn, before we leave Jesus' feeding of the 5000 and the 4000; no matter how hopeless things may look to us in the natural, if we totally give all that we have and are to God, He will take what we have in our hands and make it more than enough to meet our needs no matter how big our problems are.

The Twelve Disciples had no hope of even feeding a few of the people who were gathered to hear Jesus preach, teach and possibly work miracles. Their solution was to dismiss the crowds and let them fend for themselves. Jesus wanted them to learn that if they gave to Him whatever they had, no matter how meager it may have seemed to them, that God would take it, bless it, and make it more than enough to meet their needs, no matter how big those needs were.

This was why when Jesus blessed the bread and fish that He handed it to them. The miracle happened through their hands so that they could better understand that God is their Jehovah Jireh. He would always provide what they needed if they would just believe in Him. Jesus taught them that when they totally surrendered to Him that He would cover their needs.

That lesson is also for us, if we want to walk in God's blessings then we have to give Him all that we are; we have to become totally dependent upon Him as our Jehovah-Jireh. 2nd Corinthians 12:9 expresses it like this, *"And He said unto me, My grace is sufficient for thee: for my strength is made perfect in weakness. Most gladly therefore will I rather glory in my infirmities, that the power of Christ may rest upon me."*

CHAPTER 36

DIG INTO SCRIPTURE

To get back to the nuts and bolts of resurrecting your marriage, I cannot over emphasize that praying to God and digging into His Word is key. Get your notebook out and start writing down scriptures that speak to you and use them to pray daily. If you are having trouble getting started then take your Strong's Exhaustive Concordance and look up under the topics of: husbands, wives and marriage. If you don't have a Strong's Exhaustive Concordance yet then go to your pastor and ask if you can borrow one from your church. Or go to a public library and see if they have one in their reference section. If all else fails and they don't then sit down at a computer and type in the question "what does the Bible say about marriage, husbands or wives?" You will have plenty of information to choose from.

One word of caution here in using the internet, check your sources as to whom is writing their opinions to your questions, sometimes you will have atheists posing as being knowledgeable as to Biblical questions. Additionally, you will find people who mean well but in reality they are clueless as to what the Word of God says on any subject because they are not students of God's Word. They go on hearsay, not Biblical facts. Anytime you allow someone to speak Biblically into your life make sure that they are able to back up what they say with Scripture and verse not just opinion. To be able to speak truthfully on what is in the Bible it requires that you have spent quality time studying the Bible under the mentorship of Biblically sound teachers.

CHAPTER 37

EDUCATE YOURSELF BY READING CHRISTIAN BOOKS ON MARRIAGE

Also, during this time period an excellent and very helpful book to read is "*Love Must Be Tough*" by Dr. James Dobson (new hope for marriages in crisis). Dr. Dobson's book will help you to better understand the how and the why that your marriage got into trouble and he will give you additional tools to help heal your marriage. This is a good book to read in conjunction with going to a Christian Counselor. If you want to, the organization that Dr. Dobson started, Focus on the Family, will allow you to speak with a Christian Counselor if you request it when you call them. They do not rush you off of the phone and they will continue to help you if you ask them to.

This is a good place to start until you get established with your own local Christian Counselor. Often times they will be able to provide you with a list of Christian Counselors in your area. The people that they would be recommending to you would have to have gone through Focus on the Family's screening process and would have to meet their high standards to qualify as a recommended Christian Counselor. You will find them extremely helpful in the initial time period when you are still just trying to come to grips with what your spouse has dumped on you.

Additional resources to help you through this are any books on marriage and marriage counseling by Dr. H. Norman Wright. He is a Christian Counselor who has been in practice for over 30 years and has written at least 70 books. One that would be extremely helpful to you right now would be his "*The Marriage Checkup*" and also his "*How to Speak Your Spouse's Language.*" "*The Marriage Checkup*" can be viewed as a diagnostic tool to help you understand what is broken in your marriage relationship and how to set about fixing it. The "*How to Speak Your Spouse's Language*" book is to help you understand that your spouse and you most likely have different communication styles and how to recognize what they are and to use this knowledge to improve your communication style. Any of his books dealing with the topic of marriage will bring knowledge to you to help heal your marriage.

CHAPTER 38

DON'T EVER TAKE YOUR SPOUSE FOR GRANTED

I would also like to add here that sometimes we are all guilty of taking our spouse for granted. This lack of basic consideration for our spouse just seems to slip in sometimes while we are so busy doing everything that we need to do. We need to strive to always have a servant's heart toward our spouse. Don't take the attitude "well they are perfectly able to get their own glass of water, dinner, towel, etc, why should I be their servant?" When you constantly show kindness, love and consideration to your spouse it will come back to you tenfold.

Before you say you won't, just try it and see the wonderful results that it evokes in your spouse. Also, be polite and use your manners with your spouse. A please and a thank you are very much under-used words today that show how much you appreciate your spouse's efforts. Definitely don't forget to say you are sorry if you goofed. It will get easier with practice. We all make mistakes, so "I'm sorry" should be a readily accessible part of your vocabulary. We all know people who think that they are perfect and as such unable to make a mistake and we all know what big pains they are to everyone that they are around. Don't be that way.

Above all else, never let a day go by that you don't say "I love you" to your spouse at least several times during the day and of course seal it with a kiss. Let your spouse know how glad you are that you married them and that you would do it again in a heartbeat. Take time to show appreciation to your spouse and just like when we pray to God, take time to listen to what your spouse is actually saying; just don't discard it because you feel that you are right and they have no clue as to what they are talking about. Give their opinion the respect that it deserves because it is coming from your spouse.

If at all possible, especially when you have young ones in the home, make some time for just the two of you, even if it is just a walk around the block. Nurture and care for your relationship. Good relationships don't happen by chance, they are developed with a lot of care and feeding. God has blessed you with your spouse, say thank you to Him every day for giving them to you. Ask God to give you the wisdom and discernment to do your part in keeping your marriage strong. The book of James chapter 1, verse 5 teaches us that, *"If any of you lack wisdom, let him ask of God, that giveth to all men, liberally, and upbraideth not; and it shall be given him."* God can truly make your marriage a heaven on earth if you allow Him to.

CHAPTER 39

PRAY WITH YOUR SPOUSE

I cannot over emphasize the importance in your marriage of praying with your spouse. This is an area like saying grace before your meals; a lot of people are uncomfortable in praying with their spouse or anyone else for that matter too! They feel embarrassed by it (unless it is on a Sunday and in church with a lot of other people), so take baby steps at first. Nothing says "I love you" like taking the time to pray over or with your spouse if they are having a problem or are sick. When your spouse loves you to the point that they would set aside any personal concerns over their dignity and pride that they would come before God in all humility and submission to intercede for your needs that is a level of intimacy that few ever truly achieve. It is not impossible to do so and it makes you feel more loved than you could ever conceive of.

A praying spouse, especially over your needs gives you such a sense of security in your marriage. There is nothing that can compare to it. If you have never felt blessed by God, you will when your spouse prays over you or with you. Like a lot of the things that I have suggested, try it before you say you can't or won't go there. You just can't conceive of the level of intimacy that God will bring to your marriage. Invite Him in; you'll never go back to what you had before because you won't want to accept second best when you see all that your marriage can be in God. Here are some scriptures and ways to pray for your wayward spouse to get you started. It is certainly not the only way to pray but until you are more familiar with God's Holy Word it is a good place to start.

PRAYERS OVER A HUSBAND

1ˢᵗ Timothy 3:2-4

A bishop*
Then must be blameless,
The husband of one wife,
Vigilant, sober,
Of good behaviour,
Given to hospitality,
Apt to teach;

Not given to wine,
No striker, not greedy of filthy lucre;**
But patient,
Not a brawler,
Not covetous.

PSALM 112

Praise ye the LORD,
Blessed is the man that feareth the LORD,
That delighteth greatly in His commandments.

His seed***
Shall be mighty upon earth:
The generation of the upright shall be blessed.

Wealth and riches
Shall be in his house:
And his righteousness endureth forever.

---

*Bishop, meaning husband (refers to spiritual leadership)
**Lucre, meaning "Unhealthy obsession over money".
***Seed, meaning "children"

Unto the upright
There ariseth light,
He is gracious
And full of compassion, and righteous.

A good man showeth favour,
And lendeth,
He will guide his affairs with discretion.
Surely
He shall not be moved for ever:
The righteous
Shall be in everlasting remembrance.

He shall not be afraid of evil tiding,
His heart is fixed,*
Trusting in the LORD.

His heart is established,
He shall not be afraid,
Until he see his desire upon his enemies.

He has dispersed,
He hath given to the poor;
His righteousness endureth for ever;
His horn shall be exalted with honour.

The wicked shall see it,
And be grieved;
He shall gnash with his teeth,
And melt** away;
The desire of the wicked shall perish.

---

*Fixed, meaning "firm or set".
**Melt, meaning "to waste with disease and to faint with fatigue".

JAMES 1:12-16

*Blessed is the man
That endureth temptation:*

*For when he is tried,
He shall receive the crown of life.*

*Which the LORD hath promised
To them that love Him.*

*Let no man say
When he is tempted,
I am tempted of God:*

*For God cannot be tempted with evil,
Neither tempteth He any man.*

*But every man is tempted,
When he is drawn away of his own lust,
And enticed.*

*Then when lust hath conceived,
It bringeth forth sin;*

*And sin,
When it is finished,
Bringeth forth death.*

Do not err
My beloved brethren.*

---

*Err, meaning "to roam from the truth".

PRAYERS OVER A WIFE

Proverbs 31:10-12, 20, 25-30

Who can find a virtuous woman?
For her price is far above rubies.

The heart of her husband
Doth safely trust in her,
So that he shall have no need of spoil.*

She will do him good
And not evil
All the days of her life

She stretcheth out her hand to the poor;
Yea she reacheth forth her hands to the needy.

Strength and honour are her clothing;
And she shall rejoice in time to come.

She openeth her mouth with wisdom;
And in her tongue is the law of kindness.

She looketh well to the ways of her household,
And eateth not the bread of idleness.

Her children arise up,
And call her blessed;
Her husband also, and he praiseth her.

Many daughters have done virtuously,
But thou excellest them all.

---

*Spoil meaning "booty".

Favour is deceitful,
And beauty is vain:
But a woman that feareth the LORD,
She shall be praised.

COLOSSIANS 3:18-19

Wives,
Submit yourselves
Unto your own husbands,
As it is fit in the LORD.

Husbands,
Love your wives,
And be not bitter against them.

GENESIS 2:23-24

And Adam said,
This is now bone of my bones,
And flesh of my flesh:
She shall be called Woman,
Because she was taken out of Man.

Therefore
Shall a man leave his father
And his mother,
And shall cleave unto his wife,
And they shall be one flesh.

SCRIPTURES FOR MARRIAGES

1ˢᵗ CORINTHIANS 13:4-8

Charity*
Suffereth long,
And is kind;
Charity
Envieth not;
Charity
Vaunteth not itself,
Is not puffed up.

Doth not behave itself unseemly,
Seeketh not her own,
Is not easily provoked,
Thinketh no evil.

Rejoiceth not in iniquity,
But rejoiceth in the truth;
Beareth all things,
Believeth all things,
Hopeth all things,
Endureth all things.

Charity never faileth:
But whether there be prophecies,
They shall fail;
Whether there be tongues,
They shall cease;
Whether there be knowledge,
It shall vanish away.

*Charity (all instances), meaning "love".

ROMANS 3:23

For all have sinned,
And come short
Of the glory of God.

PROVERBS 21:19

It is better
To dwell in the wilderness,
Than
With a contentious
And an angry woman.

Father God, in the Name of Jesus Christ, I come against anything or person that gets in the way of (spouse's name) walk with God. Father God, in the Name of Jesus Christ, I place a wedge between any person or thing that keeps (spouse's name) from you. Father God, in the Name of Jesus Christ, I take that person or thing out of their life. Amen.

Father God, in the Name of Jesus, I bind (name spouse) to the place where they are bound to you Father; to bring them to their knees in total submission, obedience and repentance. Father, give them a full awareness and complete knowledge of all of the damage and pain that they have caused their family. Father, give them a contrite heart, a changed heart, and a heart, body, mind and soul that only wants to love and please you Father. Amen.

Father God, if I'm not praying correctly, please give me the right words. I will always need and want your direction in my life. Father God, in the Name of Jesus, please show me how and what I should be praying for my spouse. Amen.

Father God, in the Name of Jesus, I come against, I bind from doing harm, and I rebuke and send back to the fiery gates of hell to be destroyed forever and a day and never to rebound back against us:
1.) The ungodly relationship that my spouse is engaged in.
2.) The spirit of the adulterer that is in my spouse.
3.) The spirit of lies and deception that has beguiled my spouse.
4.) Any generational curses that have affected our family.
5.) All plans that the enemy has for us.

You can personalize this prayer to fit the needs of the situation or the person that you are praying for. These are basically just examples of how to get started and to show you how to pray against what you may be dealing with.

CHAPTER 40

GOD HAS GIVEN US THE POWER TO BIND AND LOOSEN

Sometimes we are a bit slow in getting started praying because we are awkward at finding just the right words that we need. In Matthew 18:18 Jesus Christ gives us the authority of binding and loosening, *"Verily I say unto you, Whatsoever ye shall bind on earth shall be bound in heaven: and whatsoever ye shall loose on earth shall be loosed in heaven."* With this you have God's permission to bind up evil as said here in Mark 3:27, *"No man can enter into a strong man's house, and spoil his goods, except he will first bind the strong man; and then he will spoil his house."* Here the strong man refers to Satan and any evil or entity from him. With this permission you can also bind good things to you or your family.

An example of this could be, "In the Name of Jesus Christ, I bind myself and my family into total submission, and obedience to God." You could also say something like this, "Father God, in the Name of your precious Son, Jesus Christ, I bind myself to be the best possible wife/husband to my spouse." There is no limit to what you can bind or loosen. You can use this to address lacks in your life like this, "Father God, in the Name of Jesus Christ I loosen prosperity over my family, I bind myself and my family to the prosperity that you want us to walk in so that we have enough for the needs and wants of our family and more than enough to bless others in your name. Father God, I break the curse of poverty and lack off of us." Here is a sample prayer:

Father God, in the Name of Jesus, I thank you for the privilege of taking all of my problems and concerns and placing them at the foot of the cross for Jesus to deal with. Father God in the Name of Jesus I bind myself and my spouse to walk in the marriage that you have purposed for us. Father God, in the Name of Jesus I bind up any hindrances that are standing in the way of our walking in your Will for us. Father God, I bind myself and my spouse to you in whatever way that pleases you.

Father God, I bind healing to our marriage and I ask that you rekindle the love that we felt when we first took our wedding vows before you. Father God, in the Name of Jesus Christ, I give you our hearts. Amen.

You can bind your mind, your hands, your feet and your heart to the mind, hands, feet, heart, and so on to Jesus Christ so that your life is more Christ like and to ensure that you are walking in the purpose that God has ordained for you. When you are walking in God's purpose for you then you will be walking in God's blessings for you. Dr. Sherill Piscopo of Evangel Christian Church, in Roseville, Michigan has done a fantastic teaching on "*Binding and Loosing Prayer*".

It is worth your time to dig into this topic more deeply. This teaching will greatly enhance your prayer life and it is not expensive to purchase. While you're checking out this teaching on "Binding and Loosing Prayer" it is important to know that Evangel has many excellent teaching tapes that are available to you. Evangel is also home to Destiny School of Ministry and it is a wonderful place to start your walk with God.

Finally you can pray like this:

Father God, in the Name of Jesus Christ I ask that your make a way for our marriage and family to be healed.
Father God, in the Name of Jesus Christ, I ask that you make a way that (name spouse) will fully acknowledge what they have done and to be truly repentant for it.
Father God, in the Name of Jesus Christ I ask that you make a way for me to do your will in all things.
Father God, in the Name of Jesus Christ, I ask that you make a way for (name spouse) to really value our marriage again and to honor our marriage vows.
Father God, in the Name of Jesus Christ I ask these petitions according to your Will, amen.

It is critical that when you pray in this manner you never use negatives. You would never pray that God would make a way for something bad to happen to someone. God wants us to always show Christian love to each other, even those that we don't like. His Word says it best in Matthew 5:44, *"But I say unto you, Love your enemies, bless them that curse you, do good to them that hate you, and pray for them which despitefully use you, and persecute you."*

When you pray in negative words you are getting into manipulation and witchcraft; these are things that do not have a place in the prayers of a Christian. Negative prayers are ungodly, don't ever go there. Remember, no matter how bad things may appear in the natural, God is in control of all things and He will in His perfect timing and to His Glory bring good out of what appears to us to be bad. Have faith in your Father, He will never disappoint you.

CHAPTER 41

WHAT DOES GOD SAY ABOUT DIVORCE?

What does God say about the subject of divorce? In Matthew, chapter 19, we see that God views the subjects of marriage and divorce very seriously. He has stated that once a man and a woman marry they are no longer two separate individuals anymore, they are now one flesh and that is part of why when a spouse is trying to walk away from their marriage your heart feels like it is being ripped in two. Furthermore, that one flesh should only be separated by death. God holds the sanctity of marriage so seriously that He put the only thing that could break and defile that sanctity in His Ten Commandments. Exodus 20:14 states to all, *"Thou shalt not commit adultery"* and further in Leviticus 20:10 continues with, *"And the man that committeth adultery with another man's wife, even he that committeth adultery with his neighbour's wife, the adulterer and the adulteress shall surely be put to death."*

His Word teaches us that the only form of divorce that God sanctioned was if immorality could be proved on the part of the women during the one year betrothal period where a couple was technically married by legal contract but the marriage was not yet consummated. Hebrews 13:4 states, *"Marriage is honourable in all, and the bed undefiled: but whoremongers and adulterers God will judge."* Moses instituted divorce among the Israelites in the Wilderness because so many men had disobeyed God by marrying Gentile women and the bloodline that Jesus was to come through had to be kept pure.

Additionally there is a Biblical school of thought that holds that the term immorality has additional meanings beyond sexual impurity. Some theologians hold the belief that when Jesus said that immorality was the only just cause for a divorce between His people it also included in that definition anything that is Biblically immoral. That would include a spouse who is physically and or verbally abusive; a spouse who is living an immoral and an ungodly lifestyle and wants you to participate in it with them and therefore causes you to sin. Sadly there are more atrocities in our lifestyles today than just simply committing adultery. It has become a proverbial Pandora's Box of sexual perversions and deviations that exist now and all manners of activities that are ungodly that people can justify as acceptable to do to and with each other.

Dr. Lester Sumrall in his Book *Take It...It's Yours, Seizing Your Spiritual Dominion,* speaks to God's view of sex very well.

> Sex is the most intimate relationship between humans. And only the sexual relationship has the potential for creating an immortal soul. From the beginning, God has been very protective about sex. He addressed Himself to it very clearly in His Word. God's moral nature has never altered, and He does not change His moral standards to suit a self indulgent generation.
>
> Since the Garden of Eden, Satan has sought to degrade man in the area of sex. All forms of perversion, homosexuality, and moral uncleanness are contrary to God's laws of nature.[9]

Scripture tells us that divorce is not the unforgivable sin (Matthew 12:31). So if you find that you have to go through a divorce even after everything that you have done to Biblically turn your marriage around do not sit in condemnation of yourself. Romans 8:1 teaches us, *"There is therefore now no condemnation to them which are in Christ Jesus, who walk not after the flesh, but after the Spirit."* John 5:24 further declares to us: *"Verily, verily, I say unto you, He that heareth My word and believeth on Him that sent Me, hath everlasting life, and shall not come into condemnation; but is passed from death unto life."* You have not failed. God will see you through this with His love, mercy and grace. Pick yourself up, take extra good care of your health, don't forget to eat right everyday and exercise at least three times a week. Ask people to

---

[9] Sumrall, Lester, *Take it...It's Yours, Seizing Your Spiritual Dominion* (South Bend, Indiana: Lester Sumrall Evangelistic Association, 1986), p. 41.

keep you in their prayers and above all else dig into the treasure that is God's Word; it will carry you through all of the storms of your life.

Keep your eyes on Jesus and He will repair and restore your life. He will heal the hurt and pain that you are encountering right now. He will be your comfort and your shield. Take time to mourn for what you have lost. It is okay to cry, just don't let grief and bitterness fill your heart and consume your life. Ask God to help you forgive your spouse and yourself; pray for God's blessings and purpose in your life and that of your ex-spouse.

When we totally submit ourselves to God you will find that He will keep you safe from everything that Satan throws at you. Picture yourself sitting safely in the middle of God's cupped hands. All of the forces of Hell can be breaking loose around you and you will be unharmed because you are a child of the Most High God. I have always found that if God removes a specific person or persons out of your life He has a reason for this. He will replace said person or persons with someone or something so much better.

Philippians 4:4-7 teaches us to, *"Rejoice in the LORD always: and again I say, Rejoice. Let your moderation be known unto all men. The LORD is at hand. Be careful for nothing*; but in everything by prayer and supplication with thanksgiving let your requests be made known unto God. The peace of God, which passeth all understanding, shall keep your hearts and minds though Christ Jesus."* Philippians 4:13 declares to us that, *"I can do all things through Christ which strengtheneth me."* Finally, Philippians 4:19-20 says to us, *"But my God shall supply all your need according to His riches in glory by Christ Jesus. Now unto God and our Father be glory forever and ever. Amen."*

*meaning "don't be anxious about anything"

CHAPTER 42

BASIC PRAYERS FOR DAILY LIFE

EVERYDAY PRAYERS

Abba Father,

I love you, I thank you for loving me enough to send your only begotten Son to die on the cross for me. I know now that Jesus died not only for all of the sins of the world, but for all of the sins that I have committed and will ever commit in the present and future. I know also if I want to please you I need to forgive others as you have forgiven me. I have to lay the anger and hurt down in my life. I thank you for all of the testing you have been putting me through. I know that you are in total control of all things in my life and everything will come back for your purpose and pleasure. I thank you for cleaning out the trash in my life and bringing me into a closer relationship with you.

Thank you Father for helping me back on track whenever I veer off of it. Thank you Father for keeping your hand upon me; I know that your hand upon me will bring discipline, correction and blessings to my life. Thank you for loving me enough to stretch and mold me into a child of yours that will bring you pleasure and serve your Kingdom. Father God, your Word tells us that you are the potter and we are the clay; make of me whatever vessel brings you pleasure and is useful for your Kingdom (Romans 9:21). Keep me Father even when my flesh body wants no part of being kept. Father God, I love you so very much, thank you for remembering me, in the precious Name of Jesus Christ. Amen.

PRAYER BEFORE GROCERY SHOPPING

Dear Father,

I ask for the wisdom to shop wisely for my family. I ask that you help me to make food choices that are healthy for my family (1st Corinthians 6:19-20). *I ask that you keep me from making frivolous purchases and also impulse buys. I ask that you give me the ability to stay within the grocery budget that is respectful of the money that we have as a family to spend on groceries. I ask Father, that you stretch the money that I have to do my shopping with so that I am able to purchase all of the food and other items that I need to buy today to meet my family's needs. Father, I also ask that you help me to save additional money by matching up the coupons that I have to the items that I need.*

Father, you have said that you have numbered the very hairs upon our head (Luke 12:7). *So I know that something as necessary to me and my family as grocery shopping and staying within the family's budget is also of concern to you. I thank you Father, that you love us so much that you will even bless my grocery shopping. I ask this petition in the precious Name of Jesus Christ, your only begotten Son. Amen.*

PRAYER FOR TRAVELING MERCIES

God our Father wants us to involve Him in all areas of our lives, even each and every time that we get behind the wheel of our cars (or tractors, lawnmowers or anything else that we would be driving). It is our birthright as a child of God to be able to ask for His favor over our lives and rightly expect to receive it. So, if you really think about it, a prayer asking for traveling mercies is very appropriate.

Father God, I ask for your traveling mercies as I drive today. I ask that you keep me alert to the conditions around me and that you place a hedge of protection around me with your angels. Psalm 91:11-12 declares to us, "For He shall give His angels charge over thee, to keep thee in all thy ways. They shall bear thee up in their hands, lest thou dash thy foot against a stone." I ask that you bless me with good driving skills and that you keep all people, animals and vehicles out of my pathways. I thank you for loving me enough that you care if I come and go from my home safely. Amen.

You don't have to use the same words as I have given you here. This is just to get you into the habit of asking God to bless your driving and safety for your trip and even if you only remember to ask God for "traveling mercies" you are still covered. Also, remember to thank Him for your safe passage when you are home again.

Another thought here on driving, we have all encountered drivers that exhibit extremely poor driving skills. In the natural, our first instinct may be that we yell some choice, colorful metaphors when they tail gate us or perhaps they cut us off and then slam on their brakes in front of us. I need to remind you here that God wants us to forgive these people, so if we are going to be obedient to God's Word then we are not going to fill the car with "blue statements" critiquing said person's driving abilities, choices and possibly their family heritage. This will take some practice but it is do-able, so if you stumble with this at first it will get easier and eventually you can even do it with a smile upon your face and really mean it.

So the next time someone is driving on the roadways with you and they do something really stupid and dangerous, ask God to bless them with better driving skills. At first, it may be hard to get these words of love out of your mouth (especially as you are having to slam on your brakes to keep from rear ending them) but the more that you do it, the easier it will be and the more that God will bless you because you are trying to be an obedient child to Him.

Remember that in some place and time, in our driving history, we too have been the person who sorely was in need of better driving skills. We may not have been smart enough to know that, but each and every one of us has at sometime done both stupid and dangerous things as we drive and it is ONLY by the grace and mercy of a good and benevolent God that we are here. So, again I say, try to show that same mercy and grace from God to others. We all need a bit of elastic in our lives. Romans 3:23 says it like this, *"For all have sinned, and come short of the Glory of God."* God tells us that we should be able to show forgiveness to people who sin against us seventy times seven in any given day (Matthew 18:21-22).

Before we leave this chapter it is equally important to ask God to bless our homes and property. As we leave our house it just takes about a minute to ask God to keep our homes and everything that we leave behind in our homes (including spouse, children, pets, babysitter, and possessions) and our property safe and protected so it is all there in one piece when we return home. So here is a sample prayer for you to start with and I will explain the use of praying the Blood of Jesus in the next chapter.

Father God, in the Name of Jesus I draw a blood line of protection around my home and everyone and everything in it including my spouse, children, animals, possessions, property and everything that has value to me and that I love. Father, I also ask that you set your angels round about my property to keep everyone and everything safe. Father, in the Name of Jesus I set a hedge of protection around all that I love here; thank you Father, in His precious Name. Amen.

CHAPTER 43

HOW TO PRAY USING THE BLOOD OF JESUS?

Dr. Dick Scott is a past President of Life Bible College in San Dimas, California. In his internet article entitled *"Nothing But the Blood of Jesus"* he expresses scripturally what the Blood of Jesus means to us:

> If you don't have it, you have no life - John 6:53
> If you do have it, you have eternal life - John 6:54
> You are bought with it - Acts 20:28
> You are justified by it - Romans 5:9
> You have redemption through it - Ephesians 1:7
> You're brought near to God by it – Ephesians 2:13
> You make peace with God through it - Colossians 1:20
> Your conscience is cleansed by it - Hebrews 9:14
> You have absolutely no forgiveness without it - Hebrews 9:22
> You have confidence to enter into the presence of God with it - Hebrews 10:19
> You are made holy by it - Hebrews 13:12
> You are freed from sin by it - Revelation 1:5
> And, with it you even overcome the accuser - Revelation 12:11[10]

Revelation 12:11 is a good place to start with teaching you about the authority that you have in the Blood of Jesus Christ, *"And they overcame him* (meaning Satan) *by the Blood of the Lamb, and by the word of their testimony..."* Bottom line there is good and evil in this world. To simplify, God is good and Satan is evil. The Bible tells us in John 10:10 that Satan came into this world for three purposes; to kill, steal and destroy our happiness. The Bible tells us in John 3:16, *"For God so loved the world that He gave His only begotten Son, that whosoever believeth in Him should not perish, but have everlasting life."* Hosea 4:6 tells us that: "My people perish for lack of knowledge".

---

[10] Taken from "Nothing but the Blood of Jesus", written by Dr. Dick Scott http://www.ptm.org/99PT/MarApr/NothingbutBlood.htm.

Luke 10:19 tells us that God gives us all the power that we ever need to overcome Satan and to stop him dead in his tracks, also James 4:7 teaches us on this subject, *"Submit yourselves therefore to God. Resist the devil, and he will flee from you."* The trouble is that most people remain ignorant of the fact that God has given us this power. Most churches don't bother to teach such an antiquated doctrine. They also often times fail to teach people the power that is in the Name of Jesus Christ and that is in His shed Blood. Pastor Billye Brim in her book, *"The Blood and the Glory"* expresses it this way.

> ...God showed me that Satan has systematically tried to rob from the church, truth about the Blood of Jesus and its practical use; especially as a primary weapon against him.
>
> He called to my remembrance how some years ago a major denomination took all the Blood songs out of their hymnals, with a resultant loss of power. They said the Blood frightened little children.
>
> Little children are not frightened by the joyous singing of, "There is power, power; Wonder-working power, In the Blood, of the Lamb."
>
> But someone is. Satan is.[11]

If you can think of the Blood of Jesus like this, all power is in His shed Blood from the cross, just like in the natural our life is in our blood, no blood, no life. The first time in Scripture that you will see a blood line being drawn is in the book of Exodus 12:22-23, *"And ye shall take a bunch of hyssop, and dip it in the blood that is in the basin, and strike the lintel* (meaning "top of the door frame") *and the two side posts with the blood that is in the basin; and none of you shall go out at the door of his house until the morning. For the LORD will pass through to smite the Egyptians; and when He seeth the blood upon the lintel, and on the two side posts, the LORD will pass over the door, and will not suffer* (meaning "allow") *the destroyer to come in unto your house to smite*

---

[11] Brim, Billye, The *Blood and the Glory* (Tulsa, Oklahoma: Harrison House, Inc., 1995), p. 15.

you." All of the Israelites who obeyed the Word of God and all of their possessions including their animals were safe from the destroyer.

Jesus' shed blood from the cross is what enables us to have the gift of eternal salvation. It is the gift from God that never stops giving to us. With His Blood we have forgiveness, acceptance, salvation, justification and on it goes. For the believer in Jesus Christ everything is covered by His shed Blood. There is infinite power in His shed Blood. Unfortunately, most people in this world walk in ignorance to this fact.

Even more sadly is that most churches don't bother to teach the power and authority that we, as believers, have in the Blood of Jesus. With the Blood of Jesus we share in the full inheritance that we as a child of the Most High God deserve. Through the Blood of Jesus we walk in the same Blood covenant that God made with Abraham. Our eternal inheritance is in the Blood that was shed from the cross at Calvary. God has given us everything that we need to be triumphant over Satan because Satan is a defeated foe by the Blood of Jesus. Satan knows this fact and the only thing that keeps him in power in this world is our ignorance as to who we are in Christ and the full authority that we walk in everyday.

In the book *Blessing the Next Generation* by Pastors Marilyn Hickey and Sarah Bowling we see the examples set by Jesus that blood must be shed for sins to be forgiven:

> The pattern in the Bible from cover to cover is that blood must be shed for sins to be remitted. Certainly Jesus shed His blood on the cross of Calvary and in so doing the Bible tells us He bore our sin: "For God made Christ, who never sinned, to be the offering for our sin, so that we could be made right with God through Christ" (2nd Corinthians 5:21).
>
> In all, Jesus shed blood eight times:
> 1. He prayed with such intensity in the Garden of Gethsemane blood came from the pores of His skin.

2. He was beaten with fists as part of being interrogated by the high priest, causing bruising or bleeding under the skin.
3. His beard was plucked.
4. A crown of thorns was pressed on His head.
5. His back was ripped open by both flogging and scourging.
6. His hands were nailed to the cross.
7. His feet were nailed to the cross.
8. His side was pierced with a sword.[12]

This is why when you pray over a problem or a person we can pray in full confidence that when we plead the Blood of Jesus we have what we profess in our confession of faith. Every time we leave our homes, drive our cars, see our children or spouse off, every problem or concern that we have we should be pleading the Blood of Jesus over and upon. This is how you would do it.

In the Name of Jesus Christ, I plead the Blood of Jesus over Susie, Tommy and Joe as they go to school. So that they have a safe day and return home to me with nothing missing, and nothing broken (remember Jeremiah 29:11, see page 140). *Father, I ask for your favor and blessings upon our children. Father God, in the Name of Jesus Christ I plead the Blood of Jesus over my spouse as they leave our home and go to their job. I ask that you bless them with a productive day and that everything they put their hands to be blessed. I ask for your unmerited favor upon their day. Amen.*

Father God, in the precious Name of Jesus I plead the Blood of Jesus Christ upon my home as I leave. In the Name of Jesus Christ I draw a Blood line of protection around my spouse and their job, our children, our pets, our home, our property and everything that we love and care about. Father, I thank you that you sent your only Son, Jesus to die upon the cross for me. I thank you for your undeserved mercy and grace upon me and my family and home; in His precious Name. Amen.

---

[12] Bowling, Sarah and Hickey, Marilyn, *Blessing the Next Generation* (New York, New York: Faith Words, Hachette Book Group, 2008), p. 46.

Satan cannot cross a Blood line drawn in the Name of Jesus Christ; period. Now I have dogs, big dogs; statistics show that when you have a dog in your house that they are an excellent deterrent to burglars. By the Grace of God we have never had a problem with burglars. I don't officially know how many burglars or other evils were deterred by the presence of our dogs and that is something that I will never know. I am thankful to God that our home has been kept safe and un-violated.

When you plead the Blood of Jesus and draw a blood line of protection over and around your spouse, children, pets, home, car, property and everything that you love and care about you will never know how much evil that the Blood of Jesus has kept you safe from. Just like I don't know how much evil that our dogs have kept from our door. But be assured that pleading the Blood covers you like a gigantic shield and it does keep you safe. Also be assured that evil in all shape and forms is out and about looking to devour you and your family. 1st Peter 5:8 declares it this way, *"Be sober, be vigilant; because your adversary the devil, as a roaring lion, walketh about, seeking whom he may devour."*

In the book, *"Blessing the Next Generation"* by Pastors Marilyn Hickey and Sarah Bowling give us a further understanding of this subject:

> God has given us spiritual weapons and authority to overcome the devil's attempts to devour us. He has purchased and covered us with *the Blood of Jesus;* He has given us the authority to speak in *the Name of Jesus;* and He has given us *His Word* to speak into every situation we face. At the crux of this spiritual arsenal is the assurance that it is *God's Will* for us to triumph over the attacks of the enemy and live a blessed life.
>
> In reality, Jesus has *already* sent the devil packing! Jesus laid down His life for us and then rose from the dead. Therefore, we have available "God's mighty weapons… to knock down the Devil's strongholds." Jesus has made the ultimate provision for you and your family to enjoy a robust, abundant life, a life in

which "death is swallowed up in victory" (1st Corinthians 15:54 KJV).[13]

You may question why you are still struggling with problems that you have already plead the Blood of Jesus over and I will remind you what Holy Scripture says on the subject. Isaiah 30:18, *"And therefore will the LORD wait, that He may be gracious unto you and therefore will He be exalted, that He may have mercy upon you: for the LORD is a God of judgment; blessed are all they that wait for Him."* The thought continues in Isaiah 40:31, *"But they that wait upon the LORD shall renew their strength; they shall mount up with wings as eagles; they shall run, and not be weary; and they shall walk, and not faint."* Sometimes one of the hardest things that we, as believers, have to do is to wait for God's perfect timing. Romans 8:28 teaches us this, *"And we know that all things work together for good to them that love God, to them who are the called according to His purpose."*

Be patience, the time that we spend in waiting for the LORD is time well spent. It is in the storms of life that we grow, stretch and mature in our faith walk with God. Tribulations in our life teach us patience, patience teaches us faith, as our faith grows we come closer in our personal relationship with God (Romans 5:3-5). The waiting is for a season, and at an appointed God time the waiting will be over. Ecclesiastes 3:1 confirms this for us, *"To everything there is a season, and a time to every purpose under the heaven."* Be assured, God's timing is perfect timing. So stand your Biblical ground, do not despair, continue to give Him praise and thanks, and hold fast to your faith in our LORD. Psalm 27:14 speaks to us with these words, *"Wait on the LORD: be of good courage, and He shall strengthen thine heart: wait, I say, on the LORD."* Psalm 46:10 further gives us hope in His Holy Word by this, *"Be still, and know that I am God: I will be exalted among the heathen, I will be exalted in the earth."*

---

[13] Bowling and Hickey, p. 149-150.

CHAPTER 44

PRAYING OVER THE SICK

Psalm 103:1-4

BLESS THE LORD,
O my soul;
And all that is within me,
Bless His Holy Name.

Bless the LORD,
O my soul,
And forget not
All His benefits.

Who forgiveth
All thine iniquities;*
Who healeth
All thy diseases.

Who redeemeth
Thy life from destruction;
Who crowneth thee
With loving kindness
And tender mercies.

Exodus 15:26 declares to us, *"...I am the LORD that healeth thee."* It is the Will of God that if you believe on Him you are healed. Hebrews 11:6 declares to us: *"But without faith it is impossible to please Him: for he that cometh to God must believe that He is, and that He is a rewarder*

---

* Sins

of them that diligently seek Him". 1ˢᵗ Peter 2:24 confirms this with these words: *"Who His own self bare our sins in His own body on the tree, that we, being dead to sins, should live unto righteousness: by whose stripes ye were healed."*

Dr. T. L. Osborn explains it this way in his book, *"Healing the Sick"*:

> Healing in the Bible is physical as well as spiritual.
> Sin and sickness which proliferate in the human race are both the result of the disobedience of Adam and Eve.
> The two redemptive blessings which Christ brought to the world are salvation and healing- deliverance from sin and sickness.
> Salvation from sin and sickness or healing from sin and sickness are both blessings including in our redemption, provided by one sacrifice and by one substitute. To say *healed* or to say *saved* means the same. If we say *healed*, or if we say *saved*, that is for the body as well as for the spirit.
> It would be incomplete for an unsaved person who is sick in body to be saved from sin and not be healed of sickness, after they had heard and believed this truth of the gospel.
> For you to be healed and not to be saved would be incomplete. God wants your spirit to be regenerated when your physical needs are met. Why? Because that is what redemption is. How could you be blessed physically and not be blessed spiritually, after you heard this truth? You discover Jesus as your own substitutionary sacrifice, bearing both your sins and your sicknesses in your place, and you are set free.
> This is the truth that sets people free in their bodies as well as in their spirits (John 8:32).[14]

Dr. Osborn then continues:

> The word *saved* in Romans 10:9 is the same Greek word used by Mark when he said, **as many** [sick people] **as touched Him were**

---

[14] Osborn, T. L., *Healing The Sick,* (Tulsa, Oklahoma, Harrison House, 1992), p. 26.

made whole (Mark 6:56). Both words, *saved* and *made whole*, were translated from the Greek word, *sozo*.

Each of the words found in the following scriptures are translated from the same Greek word, *sozo: healed*---Mark 5:23; *saved*---Mark 16:16; *healed*---Luke 8:36; *saved*--- Acts 2:21; *healed*---Acts 14:9; *saved*---Ephesians 2:8; *saved*---Luke 18:42; *save*---James 5:15; *made whole*--- Mark 5:34; *be whole*---Mark 5:28; *whole*---Luke 17:19; *whole*---Acts 4:9; *saved*---Acts 4:12; *made whole*---Mark 6:56. [15]

Additionally, this book of Dr. Osborn's is an excellent book to read to learn more about how God heals people. It will not disappoint you.

What all this boils down to (and I will say it again) it is God's Will that you be healed of all sickness. If you have faith in God and accept that Jesus Christ died upon the cross at Calvary for your sins then you must understand that He also healed your diseases by the stripes that He bore upon His back. It is just that simple.

There is nowhere in the New Testament that anyone (Jew or Gentile alike) who came to Jesus in faith, expecting to be healed, was turned away. He healed them all and in healing them all, He forgave their sins also. The two concepts go hand and hand and cannot be separated. Healing is the Will of God for His children. If you decide that God can't or won't heal you for whatever reason, then rest assured He won't. You have to have faith in Him, and without faith you cannot receive your healing.

It is shameful how many churches do not teach the truth of God's Word. Many people go through life thinking that God is punishing them with sickness or it's just God's Will for them to be sick. This is just not true, all sickness and disease comes from Satan, not God. If any preacher ever tries to tell you that it is God's Will that you are suffering with sickness,

---

[15] Osborn, T. L., *Healing The Sick,* (Tulsa, Oklahoma, Harrison House, 1992), p. 27.

you look them square in the eye and tell them to prove that statement in God's Holy Word. They can't.

Then you walk away from that person and their ministry and never look back. You want no part of any minister or ministry that would deliberately twist God's Words or has not taken the time to be educated in God's Word so that they can rightly discern what those precious words mean. They are bad news for anyone associated with them and they hurt God's children with their apathy and their ignorance.

Mark 16:18 states: *"they shall lay hands on the sick, and they shall recover."* James 5:14 declares, *"Is any sick among you? Let him call for the elders of the church; and let them pray over him, anointing him with oil in the name of the LORD."* It is not necessary to have the elders, pastor or priest from your church pray over sick people. You are perfectly able to do it yourself.

It does help though if you have more than one person but God does not deem that they have a religious title after their name. The prayers of regular people are heard just as well as those who have gone to theology school and maybe sometimes even better. God looks at what's in your heart, not the degree after your name. Acts 10:34 tells us *"...that God is no respecter of persons* (meaning "titles, ways of dress or what you look like"): *But in every nation he that feareth Him, and worketh righteousness, is accepted with Him."*

Laying your hand upon a sick person's forehead or your hands upon their arm or shoulders is a good way to pray over them or if there is a specific body part that has been injured then lay your hands upon it (if appropriate) and pray. Use your common sense as to when and where "laying on hands" is proper; you can also just take the person's hands and pray with them. Don't put yourself in a position where you could comprise yourself by an innocent touch being misinterpreted as sexual.

Unfortunately, with today's culture, it is a good idea to have more than one person with you while praying to act as a witness. If you know the people well this is not so important, but just use your head, you don't want to cast aspersions on your obedience to God. After you have prayed over someone who is sick and anointed them with the oil of our people, then start praising God and thanking Him. The oil of our people is 100% virgin olive oil that has been set aside for the purpose of anointing and which you have asked God to bless for this purpose.

When I say to anoint a person, I mean to take your fingertip and dip it into the oil and touch your finger tip to said person's forehead. You don't have to do anything fancy with it, just touching their forehead with the oil is okay or if you want you could make a cross with the oil on their forehead. You may not really feel like being joyous when the person still appears to be sick but God's Word tells us in Romans 4:17: *"...calleth those things which be not as though they were"* (and they will be).

This is part of your faith walk; it is hard to believe in what we can't see immediately with our eyes. Hebrews 11:1 states, *"Now faith is the substance of things hoped for, the evidence of things not seen."* 1st John 5:14, teaches us, *"And this is the confidence that we have in Him, that, if we ask any thing according to His Will, He heareth us: And if we know that He hear us, whatsoever we ask, we know that we have the petitions that we desired of Him."*

There is nothing magical about using blessed olive oil as anointing oil. This is purely an act of our faith in God and our obedience to His Word. When you anoint you are asking Jesus to do the healing. The oil does not do the healing, Jesus does. There are additional ways to use anointing oil and I will cover that a little later.

When you ask something of the Father, in the "Name of Jesus Christ" you document that you are a believer in Jesus Christ and His confession of faith. It is very important and respectful that we pray this way. The words that you use don't have to be fancy words at all. Speak from your heart, God knows what you want to say and the Holy Spirit will help you to find just the right words to speak.

It is important also to remember not to forget to open your prayer by asking forgiveness of God for your sins and also asking Him to help you truly forgive others. So, no matter what your petition is about always start your prayers in this manner. It pleases and honors our Father God. It is not mandatory that you do this but since an unforgiving heart is considered a major hindrance and blessing blocker for God to work in our lives, it is a good idea to at least go through the motions so that God can change our hearts and make them truly forgiving and loving towards all people.

Several years before my father died, he was hospitalized and in the Intensive Care Ward. His many doctors told us to round up the family for surely he was on his death bed. We all said our tearful goodbyes to Dad and because he was so sick that the hospital priest came in and gave him last rites. We waited our death vigil outside and inside of his room as space allowed for there were many of us present. Eventually some of us went home to wait for the news of his impending death; after twenty-four hours it still did not come, but what did come surprised us all.

The following morning he, on his own power took out his breathing tube from his throat, set up in bed and told his doctors and nurses that if he had his hunting rifle there he would have lined them up and shot them for worrying his family by telling people he was dying. He called them quacks and proceeded to put his kitchen order in for a ham and cheese sandwich on rye.

When my mother asked his doctors what had happened they could not explain the how and why he was doing so well and ready to go home; they had no answers. Never, never discount the power of being obedient to anoint with God's anointing oil. My father was hospitalized several more times, but each time that he was near death, and was anointed and prayed over he always made a miraculous recovery that dumbfounded the doctors.

Several years later my father did die, but it was not a long and a drawn out affair. He was not in a hospital surrounded by doctors and nurses, he was in his own home with my mom by his side and God took him home in a quick heart beat. No tubes, no IV's, no sterile and antiseptic smelling atmosphere, he was in the home that he built with his own hands, where he had lived the last 42 years of his life and where he had raised his children with a loving wife of 55½ years by his side. 1st Chronicles 16:34 speaks well to this, *"O give thanks unto the LORD; for He is good; for His mercy endureth forever."*

It is perfectly alright with God to use doctors or medicine for healing. Of the original Apostles, Luke was a medical doctor. It does not indicate a lack of faith on your part, sometimes God will heal people instantly and sometimes he will use medical doctors and modern medicine to provide the healing. Either way, still pray over someone who is sick for healing as this honors God with your obedience.

CHAPTER 45

PRAYERS TO BLESS OUR CHILDREN

It's very critical to pray over our children everyday no matter how old they may be. Scripture teaches us that words of life and death come out of our mouths (Proverbs 18:21); never, never, never speak curse words over your children no matter how angry you may be with them. I cannot emphasize how critically important it is that you don't do this. You only have to recall your last trip to the grocery store or the mall to remember an example of parents doing this.

Speaking of this subject matter brings to my mind a trip to the local grocery store in the late afternoon on a New Year's Eve. There was a young girl in braids, perhaps she was 10 or 11 years old and I kept crisscrossing carts with her in the different aisles. The entire time that I spent in the store with her she was on the verge of tears. I don't know the why of it, but her father kept yelling at her, calling her stupid, and the like. I did not hear a kind word come out of his mouth for his daughter and this was just so very sad. I have never forgotten her face and how miserable she must have felt.

When you speak curses, and I don't just mean the obvious words that we all refer to as "curse words" you are placing a curse upon your child or anyone else that you speak to like that. Now, you may be asking yourself do curses really exist today, isn't that rather antiquated thinking? Yes, curses are alive and well today in this century; they are not just a thing of our past.

Think of all of the times that you have heard people say to their children, "you're just like your father (or your mother)", "you're no good", "can't you do anything right", "I hope you have ten children just as bad as you are", "you're bad", "you're fat", "you're ugly", " no decent man will want to marry you", "you're a lazy bum" and on, and on, and on it goes. Anything negative that you speak to and over your children or anyone else is a curse on them. The words that a parent speaks over their offspring should be positive and edifying words.

Right now, it is possible that you're thinking this is a bit unrealistic. Unless you change your thinking it will remain impossible to do. Romans 12:2 speaks very clearly to us on the subject: *"And be not conformed to this world: but be ye transformed by the renewing of your mind, that ye may prove what is that good, and acceptable and perfect, Will of God."* How can we renew our minds to change our negative way of thinking? We can renew our minds by seeking God's Wisdom and studying His Holy Word.

We can speak scripture over our children such as Jeremiah 29:11, *"For I know the thoughts that I think toward you, saith the LORD, thoughts of peace, and not of evil, to give you an expected end."* At first this scripture may not sound very appropriate but when you look up the meaning of the word peace you get a different perspective. When we need to find out what a word in the Holy Bible means we do not go to a regular dictionary, we go to a Bible Dictionary.

The one that I prefer is called "The New Strong's Exhaustive Concordance of the Bible." This is an excellent tool to have in your personal library in addition to an original "King James Bible." The original King James is the only Bible that you can take all of the words that are in it, with the help of your Strong's Concordance, and find out what they meant in the original language that they were written in.

So let's look closer at what the word "peace" means in this verse. When you look it up, you will find that it means nothing missing, nothing broken, whole, good health, prosperity, safe, happy, and favor. Expected means very much the same today as it did in Biblical times, i.e., expectation, hope, live, thing that I long for. So, when we pray this scripture over our children we are asking God to bless them and make them healthy with nothing missing, nothing broken and a happy and a prosperous future.

Let us return to the how of praying over our children no matter how old they may be. If your child is sickly, then you are going to first ask God to heal whatever the problem is with your child. Then you are going to thank Him and praise Him for healing your child. It doesn't matter if you can't see it manifested immediately. What does matter is that your faith is strong enough to profess that God has healed your child.

Also, have praise music or regular hymns playing in the background. It doesn't have to be played loudly but at least have it as background music. It will help with the atmosphere in the house and it will keep the devil at bay. Remember, Satan hates hearing anyone praise God. Using God's own words to pray over any situation is excellent; you can do this by saying, "It is written in Your Word, and Your Word is always true. I am holding You to the promises that You have given me in Your Holy Word, Father."

One of the ways that you can find appropriate scriptures to pray over your child is to use your Strong's Concordance. Words are listed in it by alphabetical order; and every single word that is used in the King James Bible is listed in it. So if I had a sick child I would possibly look under the subject matter of children, health, maybe even sickness to see what God's Word says on the subject; and it will tell you where to find every scripture in the Bible. At some point you are going to find scriptures that you will feel apply to your own situation. You then use them to pray over your child, such as 1st Peter 2: 24, *"Who His own self bare our sins in His own body on the tree that we, being dead to sins, should live unto righteousness: by whose stripes ye were healed."*

Additionally *"Scripture Keys for Kingdom Living"* by June Newman Davis is an excellent source to use, but especially so if you are still new to learning how to use God's Words. She has listed a good portion of the more commonly used scriptures by different topic matters. You will find such topics as how to pray healing prayers for different illnesses and scripture on trusting God, dealing with fear, wisdom and much, much more. The book is another excellent tool to have to help you get more familiar with using God's Word in prayer.

You could possibly pray over your child like this:

Father God, it is written in your word that by your stripes we are healed (Isaiah 53:5). *Your word says that we have not because we ask not* (James 4:2-3). *Your word says that we should ask and you will give it to us* (Matthew 7:7-8). *You know that my child is sick with (specify here) a bad cold (for example). I ask Father for complete healing as is promised in Your Word for my child. I ask that his body line up in agreement with your word.*

I ask Father God, in the precious Name of Jesus Christ that the devourer be rebuked in my child. I bind my child to the health that you have said my child is to have in your precious word. I ask Father God for the favor that you have promised in your word for my child. Your word teaches me that nothing is impossible with my God, so I am asking for complete healing for my child; from the top of his head to the soles of his feet.

Your word teaches us that it is your plan that my child grows up healthy and strong with nothing missing, nothing broken (Jeremiah 29:11). *I stand upon your promises for my child, Father God. I plead the Blood of Jesus Christ over the health of my child. Thank you Father God, for my child's healing. I thank you that by Your Word and the shed Blood of Jesus that my child is healed, nothing missing, nothing broken; in the precious name of Jesus Christ. Amen.*

Don't forget to pray every day over your child to ask God to bless them with good health, strong bones, a heart and a mind that loves the LORD, an attitude of respect and honor for their parents, good grades, etc. If you see a problem area in your child don't speak negative words about it, speak positively. For instance, if your child is struggling in school in science, speak prayers about the situation this way:

"Father God, I ask that you bless my child with good skills in science class, and that you give him wisdom and understanding in this subject matter. I thank you that he is an excellent student in this area and all of his other classes."

So maybe it's not science class, maybe it is the class bully picking on him. Then you are going to pray this way;

"Father God, I ask for your favor and blessings for my child. Father God I ask that you place a hedge of protection around my child. I ask that you place your angels around about my child to keep him safe throughout his day. I ask that you make a way for the issues that are between my child and Bobby, the class bully, to dissipate. I ask that you would bless Bobby and help him to deal with why he feels the need to pick on other children. Reveal and heal the hurts that are in this child Father God; be his strength and his comfort, his fortress and his shield. Father God, show this young man your love and mercy. I ask this in the Name of your precious Son, Jesus Christ. Amen."

Ask the Holy Spirit to help you with the words. He will give you the right words to pray with. Speak from your heart, God will hear you.

One other point here is that I asked God to place a hedge of protection around my child. This is one of the ways that we Biblically have to ask God to protect us or anything else that we care about. Another way is to ask God to place angels around a person or a place. Always ask God to have His angels intervene for you in whatever way that they can. Remember that in Psalm 91:11-12 God's Holy Word teaches us this on His angels, *"For He shall give His angels charge over thee, to keep thee in all thy ways. They shall bear thee up in their hands, lest thou dash thy foot against a stone."* God's angels are around about us more than we could ever realize.

CHAPTER 46

HOW CAN WE BE SURE WHAT THE WORD OF GOD SAYS?

There is a scripture in 2nd Timothy 2:15 that goes like this: *"Study to show thyself approved unto God, a workman that needeth not to be ashamed, rightly dividing the word of truth."* I hear people repeatedly say that they have read the Bible and there is nothing much to it. Yes, you can read the Bible as just a nice story and get just that much out of it.

You can scratch the surface and get more out of it. Or you can take the time and respect that it deserves and really dig into it and find out why people who study the Bible say that the Word of God is pregnant. You can study the Bible everyday for 50 years and still find new revelation in a verse that you have read and studied countless times. The closer you come to God the closer He will come to you and the more that He will reveal to you.

Luke 14:26 is a prime example of why it is so very critical that you know what the words mean in scripture. It says, *"If any man come to me, and hate not his father, and mother, and wife, and children, and brethren, and sisters, yea, and his own life also, he cannot be My disciple."*

That doesn't sound quite right; does God really expect us to "hate" our family? No, God commands us to love one and another. Ephesians 6:1-3 declares this: *"Children, obey your parents in the LORD: for this is right. Honour thy father and mother; which is the first commandment with promise; That it may be well with thee, and thou mayest live long on the earth"* (also see Exodus 20:12, and Deuteronomy 5:16).

Additionally 1st John 4:7-8, 11-12 teaches us, *"Beloved, let us love one another: for love is of God; and everyone that loveth is born of God, and knoweth God. He that loveth not knoweth not God; for God is love…Beloved, if God so loved us, we ought also to love one another. No man hath seen God at any time. If we love one another, God dwelleth in us, and His love is perfected in us."* When you look up the definition of hate in your Strong's Concordance you will find that in this verse hate means "love less".

Now, the verse makes much more sense; we should love God more than anyone or anything in this world. If you really want to make the most of your Bible study time, then you are going to have a Strong's Concordance to help you understand the meaning of the words. It is an invaluable tool for Bible Study.

An additional question that you may have here is: "How can I speak so assuredly that the Holy Bible is the unadulterated God-Breathed and God-Inspired Word of God?" Aside from the fact that I have a deep and personal relationship with my Father God; I have personally witnessed miracles in my life and my family's life. Additionally I have a strong faith and belief in my Father God but there also is the Massorah.

The Massorah is an exact way that the original sacred texts were recorded, secured and protected. This project was started about 400 B.C. The original group of men who did this work were called the Sopherim, from the root word Saphar, meaning to count or number. This original work took about 110 years (410-300 B.C.) and was supervised by Nehemiah and Ezra. After this group finished the original securing and setting in order of the Sacred Scriptures; the scriptures were then turned over to another group of men called the Massorities and they then became the official group that were entrusted to protect it.

The Massorah is called "A Fence to the Scriptures" and Massorah comes from the root word "Masar" which means to deliver something into the hand of another. The Massorah with all of its strict rules on how scripture is to be written down, virtually locks in the meaning of the scriptures so that men cannot tinker with them. Included in this is how many letters can be in each line (30), how many lines can be in a given column (no less than 48, no more than 60), and on each page there would be a painfully exact copy (checked and double checked) of the Holy Scripture written down.

On the right side of the scripture and then also on the left side of the same scripture there would be recorded such things as how many times the letter "A" was used in each chapter. Also on either side of the Holy Scripture you would have how many times a certain word would be used in a certain chapter, how many verses are in each chapter, what the middle word is for each verse and so on and so on.

It is a very exact method of securing the integrity of the Holy Scriptures. This is just the basic information on the Massorah, there is much more to be studied if you choose to go deeper in your study of it. The point is protecting the validity of God's Holy Scriptures has been a concern for a long time and people have addressed it to the best of their abilities.

Author Josh McDowell in his book, *"A Ready Defense"*, explains what it means when people say that the Bible is inspired:

> Two important verses speak to the heart of the matter: 2nd Timothy 3:16 and 2nd Peter 1:21. The former reads: "All Scripture is inspired by God and profitable for teaching, for reproof, for correction, for training in righteousness" (NASB). The word *inspired* is a translation of the Greek word *theopneustos,* meaning God-breathed. Thus the origin of Scripture is God, not man; it is God-breathed.
>
> The second verse, 2nd Peter 1:21, says, "For no prophecy was ever made by an act of human will, but men moved by the Holy Spirit spoke from God" (NASB). This also confirms that the writers were moved by God to record that which God desired. Mechanical dictation was not employed, as some claim. Rather, God used each individual writer and his personality to accomplish a divinely authoritative work.
> The process of inspiration extended to every word ("all Scripture"), refuting the idea of myth and error. Since God is

behind the writings, and since He is perfect, the result must be infallible. If it were not infallible, we could be left with God-inspired error.

Sometimes it is easier to understand the concept of inspiration when it is compared with revelation. *Revelation* relates to the origin and actual giving of truth (1st Corinthians 2:10). *Inspiration,* on the other hand, relates to the receiving and actual recording of truth. Inspiration means that "God the Holy Spirit worked in a unique supernatural way so that the written words of the Scripture writers were also the Words of God."

The human authors of Scripture wrote spontaneously using their own minds and experiences, yet their words were not merely the words of men but actually the words of God. God's control was always with them in their writings with the result being the Bible --- the Word of God in the words of men.[16]

This is again why I recommend studying from the original King James Bible and Strong's Concordance. Meanings of words have changed over the years and if you do not know what the proper meaning of a word is, you cannot properly understand the scriptures. You just have to look back a generation or two to see how vastly some wholesome words have changed to have a perverse meaning in the common vernacular.

There is nothing wrong if you have other versions of the Bible that you like to read or even study from. A lot of people have several different versions of the Bible that they will compare the way it is written to help them understand the bigger picture. Just keep in mind that if you are using another version of the Bible you really need to study scripture first from the King James so that you have the best possible foundation to understand scripture from.

---

[16] McDowell, Josh and Wilson, Bill, *The Best of Josh McDowell, A ready Defense* (Nashville, Tennessee: Thomas Nelson, Inc., 1993), p. 175-176.

The study of scripture is not to be taken lightly. Again, 2nd Timothy 2:15 confirms this for us, *"Study to show thyself approved unto God, a workman that needeth not to be ashamed, rightly dividing the word of truth."* Further scripture states in Luke 4:4, *"...It is written, that man shall not live by bread alone, but by every Word of God."* Finally in John 8:32 we find, *"And ye shall know the truth, and the truth shall make you free."*

If you unintentionally, misinterpret scripture you can really get lost and even with the best of intentions you can be responsible for leading others astray in God's Word. A large part of why so many religious cults get started is because people have not rightly interpreted the Word of God. One of the main tools that a cult uses is language. They may use the same words that you do, but the meaning of them is totally different and that is part of the deliberate deception to mislead people.

CHAPTER 47

PRAYING OVER STRONGHOLDS

Sometimes we are all faced with serious problems that, in the natural, we have no idea how to get a handle on and no matter how hard we try we repeatedly fail at trying to correct the situation. This continual cycle of attempt and failure is very frustrating to all of us. No matter how perfect other people may appear from the outside, everyone struggles with something. These problems that are chronic to us and that we daily fail in our attempt to bring change to or to correct are called "Strongholds".

A stronghold is a fortified place that Satan builds to exalt himself against the knowledge and plans of God. There are different types of strongholds, for our purposes here we are concerned with personal strongholds and strongholds of the mind. A personal stronghold is things that Satan builds to influence one's personal life, personal sin, thoughts, feelings, attitudes and behavior patterns. A stronghold of the mind is a mindset impregnated with hopelessness, that causes the believer to accept as unchangeable something that he or she knows is contrary to the Will of God.

Satan uses these strongholds to keep us distracted from our purpose in God and disheartened by trying to make us feel like failures. How can we tell other people to pray to God to solve their problems when we appear to be just treading water where our personal problems are concerned? How can we effectively witness for God when our lives are so obviously out of His order? We need to deal with strongholds because if we don't, then we are rendered impotent for God and impotent in our usefulness for His Kingdom building.

So if a stronghold is one of Satan's strong points in our personal lives how do we handle it? First and foremost we take it to God. This is one of those areas that we may need to have others that are stronger in their faith walk actually intercede and pray over us for it to be broken. Before you get to that step where you would need to seek additional intercessory help, give it to God in prayer and with God's help try to break it yourself. If you find that you can't; it's okay. There is no shame in seeking out those prayer warriors that are stronger than you and have more prayer victories under their belts. The main concern is that it is broken, not necessarily how or who is responsible for the breaking of it.

An example of a personal stronghold would be an addiction. We all know of people who have suffered from a drug or an alcohol addiction and they have been successful in kicking it themselves without any outside help. It is wonderful if they have been successful. For the most part these types of serious addictions need a miracle from God or professional intervention to be broken. But what about the addictions in everyday life that are socially acceptable ones, like cigarettes, food, computer chat rooms, soap operas, sports, candy, soda pop and on the list goes?

Can you break these type of addictions on your own? Yes but most of us can't or aren't strong enough on our own. Some of these problems start out very innocuously and after a while we are like the frog in the pan on the stove. He had no problem sitting in the pan while the water was cold and even when it warmed up a bit, but by the time it was boiling he was too far gone to be able to help himself. Most times when we are in the middle of a personal stronghold we need additional help, but not always, so do try to take it to God first. Don't be embarrassed to ask for prayerful help if you find you aren't achieving the results that you want.

This is a sample prayer that you can personalize for your own needs.

Father God, I come before you with a broken and a contrite heart. I have struggled daily with this (name the problem). I know that on my own I am unable to overcome this. I have to have your grace and mercy to conquer this (name problem). I ask that you give me the wisdom to see what the hidden source of my chronic problem is. I ask that you help me to stop just putting a band-aid on it and actually take a spiritual axe to it and kill the source of it. I ask that you reveal and heal the source of the hurt that is feeding this chronic problem and allowing it to fester in the depths of my soul. Father God, I do not want to walk outside of your precious Word. I bind myself in every way possible to you so that I bring pleasure to you as your child. I ask that you give me the strength and the knowledge to Biblically deal with this issue that has dogged me for so many years. Amen.

Father God, I break any and all curses, hexes and vexes that are the original source of this problem. I rebuke Satan and all of his works that are in play with this problem. I rebuke any authority that I may have inadvertently given to Satan and any other familiar spirits to dwell within me. I rebuke and I send back to the sender any curses, vexes, or hexes that someone may have deliberately sent my way. Let him who loves curses receive them back. I want no part of any thing that brings you displeasure my Father God. I love you with my whole heart and being. I bind myself into total submission and obedience to you always even when my flesh doesn't want to be kept. Amen.

I thank you Father God for loving me so very much that you sent your only begotten Son to die for my sins. Father God, I surrender all that I am and all that I ever will be to you and your perfect Will for my life. I don't care how you mold this clay, as long as I serve your purpose for your Kingdom. Thank you that you see the value in me even when I repeatedly fail to please you. I thank you for your unmerited mercy and grace that you show me every day of my life. And I plead the shed Blood of Jesus upon my situation. I ask all these things in the precious Name of Jesus Christ. Amen.

CHAPTER 48

HOW TO USE ANOINTING OIL FOR ADDITIONAL BLESSINGS

Passover is a good time to bless and then each year after; re-bless your home and your vehicles. Some people prefer the New Year, either way you should do this at least once a year and sometimes more if a good reason presents itself. A good reason would be if someone comes into your home and later you find out that this person is involved in unsavory activities. Or someone brings an additional guest into your home and your discernment tells you that something is not right with this person, by all means re-bless your home.

The same thing with your car, maybe you gave a ride home to one of your children's classmates and you either learn additional information about said child or you just don't feel right about them. The more time that you spend in God's Holy Word the greater that you will find your discernment over spiritual matters will grow. This blessing will keep evil out of your home and car but sometimes we will mistakenly invite evil into our lives without being aware that we have.

When you are saying the following prayer over your house you will take your anointing oil and make a cross over the entry ways of your home. You can also do this on either side of the doorways too. I always anoint first and then I speak the blessing over the house while I touch the doorway. For the cars or any other drive-able machinery that you have on your property I make a cross on the front of the vehicle and then while touching it, I speak the blessing out loud.

You may question the wisdom of why it is necessary to bless the tractor, lawnmower or any other tool that may be used on your property. It is simply this, you ask God to bless this so that no one gets hurt with these items and it runs well. If it has moving parts to it, there is always a chance that someone can be injured while the item is in use and by blessing it you are asking God for favor and safety with its usage.

Take for example a chainsaw; it is a wonderful tool that saves men both time and back breaking labor to achieve the desired end of cutting down a tree. A chainsaw doesn't care what it cuts, it just performs its job well and cuts whatever gets in its way and when human misjudgment and chainsaws come together it is not pretty. You don't have to do any of these blessing but God gives us tools to help us and these are some of the tools that He has given to us for our betterment.

One other way that you can use anointing oil in your home is if you have a sick pet or even if a machine is acting up. Here again there is nothing magical about this oil, it is an act of faith and belief in God and an acknowledgement that He is in control of all things in our life. So when we anoint we are asking God to make things right in our life or our family's, to heal those that are ill and in the case of machinery or vehicles that they work well and safely.

Your children will get accustomed to your anointing things and people in your home. When our youngest was in college and studying for a degree in mathematics she had a particularly hard course in Calculus Based Statistics. So the first weekend that she came home the book came home and she asked if I would anoint it so that she would be successful in understanding the class. She now teaches math at a college level. Maybe one of the lessons that we should learn from using anointing oil is simple obedience to God and that we never put limits on what our God can do in our lives if we are in obedience and submission to Him.

CAR OR HOUSE BLESSING

Father God
In the Name of Jesus Christ,
I bind Satan
And the forces of darkness
From this house/car.

Father God,
I rebuke Satan
And all forms of evil
From this house/car.

Father,
In the Name of Jesus
I send them back
To where ever they came from
And not allow them
To rebound back against us.

Father God,
In the Name of Jesus Christ,
I condemn them
To wonder in the dry spots
Until they become as smoke over the pit.

In the Name of Jesus Christ,
By the authority
That you have given us
I declare that
This house/car
Be filled with the presence of the Holy Spirit
Whose power is greater than Satan's.

In the Name of Jesus Christ,
I declare that
This house/car is blessed by God
And all who dwell/drive
And enter therein
To adhere to God's Holy Commandments.

Our Father has said
That we are to be
Both salt and light onto this earth.

I ask that you send
Your Holy Angels
To place a hedge of protection
Around this house/car.

I draw a Blood Line
Of protection
In the precious Name of Jesus Christ,
Around this house/car,
To keep it safe at all times from the enemy,
And all plans that he has to come against me or my family.

We ask
That God protect us
And keep us holy
In thought, word, and deed.

In the precious Name
Of Jesus Christ of Nazareth
We pray.

Amen.

CHAPTER 49

A BIBLICAL HANDLE FOR YOUR TEENS AND PRETEENS

It is critical that you as parents set appropriate behavioral boundaries for all of your children, no matter how young or old they may be. Scripture teaches us in Proverbs 29:15 and 17 that, *"The rod and reproof give wisdom: But a child left to himself bringeth his mother to shame...Correct thy son, and he shall give thee rest; Yea, he shall give delight unto thy soul."* We all need boundaries in our life; boundaries give structure, safety and security in our lives and keep chaos at bay. A good illustration of this is how smoothly traffic would not flow if the world lacked traffic lights.

For the most part, we all have to obey the laws of the land and of society to be able to function in this world. You do your children a great disservice when you let them set their own rules. They lack the maturity to set wise and safe boundaries. We have all seen children that are in desperate need of discipline and sadly are lacking it. Children that have been raised up without the benefit of having discipline in their lives are at a disadvantage in the real world. They struggle with the rules of society because they have never been told that the rules also apply to them and that they are expected to adhere to them. When parents fail to discipline their children it is a guaranteed recipe for disaster.

As parents you can pretty much adapt this aforementioned prayer to teenagers that are painful to be around. You don't have to say to them that you are going to anoint their rooms, or their pillows and bed frame, their school books, their cell phone and iPod, computer and game stuff, and even the teenager themselves when they are sleeping soundly, Mom and Dad you get the idea. Whatever their hands touch anoint and pray over and plead the Blood of Jesus over them that God will help them to settle down and be obedient, respectful and submissive children; that they will be a blessing to your household and a pleasure when they come through the door of your home.

There is an old saying that everyone brings pleasure to a room, some when they come in the room and some when they leave the room. Here again, the best prayer will come naturally in your own words and from the depths of your heart to God. Ask the Holy Spirit to give you the right words, you can't go wrong. Another point here is your prayers will be more effective if both parents pray over this situation together. It is okay if just one parent does this but it is so much better if Mom and Dad are on the same page with this. This all goes right back to Biblical Headship in the home; Dad should be the one leading the prayers for his family as this pleases God.

I cannot leave this subject area without a serious charge to all parents that it is their responsibility to censor what their children are seeing and listening to and who their friends are. Your job is to be their God given parent, not their best buddy. If you don't take the time to get to know the environment that your child walks in and your children's friends then you are being a lazy and a neglectful parent and you will reap what you have sown.

Children do not have the maturity to judge well the people that they are associating with. Get to know the people that they call friends and maybe even more importantly get to know the parents of these young ones. It doesn't matter how much your children protest about invasions of their privacy or you just don't understand their needs and how old fashion can you get. Your kids don't know that they don't know, and it is your job as a parent to protect them from ungodly friends, music, movies, T.V. shows and so forth.

Don't fall back on the excuse that they are going to have to integrate with the real world at some time, so why not now. The why not now is that as children, all of the nerve ending and brain connections that will give them the ability to judge things wisely are not even finished connecting yet in their brains; that is especially why teenagers do such foolhardy and dangerous things. It is like expecting an eight year old to have perfect handwriting, they physically can't because all of the connections in their hands and brains are not finished developing yet.

It's expecting a cake that is not done baking to taste right; it needs more time in the oven. You cannot under estimate the influence of teenage hormones going crazy, paired with a large lack of maturity on the part of your teenager. If you don't have any gray hair by the time your child turns thirteen, be assured you will by the time they get their driver's license.

Expect your teenagers to dramatically kick and scream, if they didn't they wouldn't be normal and don't expect a thank you until they are much older and are dealing with a similar situation with their own teenagers. It will eventually come to them that there was wisdom in how they were raised. You will also be surprised at how many of their friends will come back to visit you and your spouse. You may even hear from them that your home was the one that they always knew what the rules were and that it provided them emotional security where none existed in their own home.

Mom and Dad, if at all possible, please give serious thought to home schooling your children. You may be thinking you are not qualified to do this, but before making that judgment, seek out and speak to other home schooling parents. You may find that you are better equipped than you realize to teach your children. A good place to start is to look over the ABEKA home schooling program. It is a God centered traditional based education program from Kindergarten through 12th grade. So much of the alienation and disrespect for authority that our children walk in, comes from the public schools that they attend. Don't worry that your children won't gain the necessary socialization skills by being home schooled. They will get plenty of it between church activities and also participating with other home schooled families in your area.

Another excellent resource to use is the *American Heritage Teaching Series* from David Barton. He is a Christian Historian and this ten DVD set is an excellent starting place to learn what the Christian Heritage of the United States is. You will be surprised at how much of our Christian heritage has been hidden and thus stolen from us by the school systems.

Before the 1920's our complete Christian heritage was taught even in all public schools. Starting with using the Bible to teach children their ABC's, Christian morals and values were taught in all grades and schools. But during the 1920's our American history books were rewritten by three atheists and they refocused our history off of our Godly heritage and instead only focused on the economics of our history. "The philosophy of the school room in one generation will be the philosophy of government in the next" (Abraham Lincoln).

The Supreme Court Justices that took God out of our classrooms in the early 1960's and legalized abortion in the 1970's stem from this change in how students were taught our American History. In my home state, after September 11, 2001, there were high schools that decided it was not important to make the American History class a requirement for graduation. Instead they encouraged a class that portrays America and American values as being to blame for a large portion of the problems of the world. The school superintendent and school board saw nothing wrong with this change in their curriculum.

Think back to the major problems that principals had to deal with before God was taken out of our schools; they were mainly gum chewing, talking in class and possibly smoking if the students were really bad. Unfortunately, nowadays pregnant moms and day cares for their children are not uncommon in public schools. Planned Parenthood's mini clinics, condoms being given out daily (and being sanctioned by the superintendent's office, especially around prom time), and dances where students are simulating sex acts on the dance floor raise few eyebrows from anyone and the adults that are supposed to be chaperoning, just stand by and watch.

Teachers having sex with their underage students, and guns and assaults on both students and teachers are not out of the ordinary in the classrooms. What has happened to our schools? The main change is that God was kicked out of our school systems in the early 1960's and our Christian Heritage has stopped being taught to our children.

Being a good parent is not just saying NO. Give your children acceptable outlets for their energies and don't forget to include chores. Being responsible for chores around the house helps build character and a sense of duty to family. Be the parents that are always the ones to do the chaperoning and the driving. Volunteer at their school; get to know their environment away from home. Know the adults that they interact with and that are influencing them. Be the mom and dad that say, "Yes you can have your friends over for a bon fire, barbeque and or a sleep over." Be very watchful for drugs and alcohol, they can easily be camouflaged. Even the best kid can get snared into trying them.

Find age appropriate activities to keep your children engaged and invigorated and don't forget to routinely turn off the T.V. and pull a family game out of a box to be played at the kitchen table. You just might be pleasantly surprised to rediscover the lost art of conversation with your children.

Traditional family activities such as bowling, roller skating, museums and miniature golf are still fun things to do as a family and are not extremely expensive; and if the budget is tight than maybe they would be a once a month special outing for the family. Most cities have YMCA's and they usually will offer a low cost family fare. Family unity can be enhanced greatly if you limit the after school activities to one activity per child per week. It is not necessary that your child be in every sport or music class at one time. Let them choose what is most important to them to do.

No matter how sophisticated our children think that they are, they still need time to just be kids and play, especially outdoor games. I'm not speaking to childhood games like Duck-Duck-Goose, although there is nothing wrong with traditional childhood games if this is the age of your children. Physical activity should be a part of all of our lives to be healthy and respectful of the temple that God has given us. Dad and Mom, you set the example for how your children will view exercise; so pick up a basketball, tennis racket, football, and or softball. Do whatever it takes to teach your children that exercise is important and enjoyable.

Above all else, say grace with them at your dinner table every meal and take them to church; if possible more than just on Sunday. The book of Ephesians 6:4 expresses it like this, *"And, ye fathers provoke not your children to wrath: but bring them up in the nurture and admonition of the LORD."* Look for a church that is Biblically sound for your family with lots of wholesome activities for your children to choose from and adult programs that will enrich your knowledge of God, your personal relationship with God, and your prayer life. The focus of the church should not be on "traditions of men" but on the Word of God. Keep in mind that Jesus said in Mark 7:13, "…traditions of men make void the Word of God."

Returning to the subject of preteens and teenagers, it is critical that you as parents be the ones to provide Godly information on sexual subjects to your children. Don't think that just because they haven't asked you any questions that they are not thinking about the subject of sex. Sex is all over the place, it is used to sell products from toothpaste to socks.

Your child is surrounded by both subliminal and overt sexuality every day, 24/7. Scripture teaches us in Isaiah 54:13 that, *"And all thy children shall be taught of the LORD; and great shall be the peace of thy children."* Mom and Dad, you are your child's first and best teacher. You either will step up to the plate and share God's plan of the precious gift of sexuality with your children or you will abandon them to the filth of the secular world that teaches them to rid themselves of their virginity as soon as possible.

If you are unsure where to start, then buy your children some quality Christian books on the subject and read them together and discuss what you have read. Impart your values and morals to your children; don't leave such a critical job to their friends or the schools. Here are several titles and authors of books dealing with all aspects of sexual education and purity for your children. Take a good look at these and determine which ones are age and maturity appropriate for your children.

Two books by Dannah Gresh are *"And the Bride Wore White,"* and *"The Secret Keeper, the Delicate Power of Modesty."* Another book by Dannah Gresh and Nancy Leigh DeMoss is *"Lies Young Women Believe."* *"Dateable: Are You? Are They?"* written by Justin Lookadoo and Hayley Morgan. *"The Technical Virgin: How Far Is Too Far?"* and *"Sexy Girls: How Hot is Too Hot?"* Both books are by Hayley Morgan. These will get you started and these authors do have more books on these topics available to you.

If you need more incentive to handle this subject yourselves then take the time to read two extremely well done books by Dr. Melvin Anchell, *"What's Wrong with Sex Education?"* and *"What's Wrong With Sex Education?: Preteen and Teenage Sexual Development and Environmental Influences."* Both of these books deal with the serious problems associated with the how and when sex education is presented to children in the school systems.

You may be only able to find these books online. They were both written in 1991 and the information in the books still applies today. They will definitely give you a handle on the subject and help you as a parent to understand how critical your role as your child's first sexual education teacher is. The book of Proverbs speaks to this very well too in chapter 22:6, *"Train up a child in the way he should go: and when he is old, he will not depart from it."*

Daily strive to keep the doors and windows of communication with your teenager wide open. It's hard to do especially when they want to talk at 2:30 A.M. and you're dead tired, but it will pay off in the long run. I can't honestly say that I always saw eye to eye with my teenagers but when push came to shove they brought to me what was heavy on their hearts.

An example of this is when our one daughter was fourteen and she found out that her best friend was trying very hard to get pregnant with the son of one of the teachers at our Christian School. She didn't really know what to do with this information. When she shared it with me, as the adult in the situation I knew what I had to do.

It did not make her popular with her friend and she even lost this girl as her best friend when I told her mother what was going on. Her mother and father never spoke to me after that but their fourteen year old daughter did not get pregnant that year. The young man's parents were extremely grateful that I had spoken up. Their hot romance was quickly frozen and limitations that were not put upon this young couple in the beginning were instantly installed.

It's not always just matters of sex that come up with our children. When our son was a teenager we did not make his best friend particularly happy when we shared with his parents that he was trying to emulate his favorite rock star by lighting his socks and his leather pants on fire. His goal was to start with his socks first and then work up to the leather pants. Well the plan was to totally saturate the socks with water and then pour rubbing alcohol on them and light them, which he did. The socks didn't look too bad so the next part of the experiment was to proceed to the leather slacks. He ended up jumping into his swimming pool to put the fire out of the pants. His Mom and Dad were not happy with this news, but were grateful to be able to put a stop to this before their son burned more than just his dignity.

CHAPTER 50

HOW TO TELL A GOOD MINISTER FROM A BAD MINISTER?

Be aware, that there are some churches that teach that traditions of men are equal with the Word of God. This is blasphemy against God and it is deliberately taught ignorance of God's Holy Word. Remember, Hosea 4:6 teaches us, *"My people are destroyed for lack of knowledge: because thou hast rejected knowledge, I will also reject thee, that thou shalt be no priest to me: seeing thou hast forgotten the law of thy God, I will also forget thy children."* 1st Peter 4:17 strongly tells us that God's judgment begins at the pulpit, so all of those ministers that are deliberately misleading their flocks with false doctrines, are accountable for each and every sheep that they have led astray. Any minister that is walking in this sin will have very serious consequences to deal with from God.

If you are walking in the calling of a minister or any teacher of God's Word, then it is critical that you seriously heed God's direction on this subject as given to us in 2nd Timothy 2:15, *"Study to show thyself approved unto God, a workman that needeth not to be ashamed, rightly dividing the word of truth."* Also ask for a "Statement of Faith" from the church office.

A "Statement of Faith" is an official list of what the church's denominational beliefs are. If the beliefs of this church are in agreement with God's Word - great; if not, give serious consideration of the points that you disagree on. Then after prayerful consideration, let God guide you to stay or move on. Sometimes God will have you stay in a situation like this, so as to help others find the truth, so don't just rush out of the door without seeking God's Wisdom and direction on this matter.

The way to tell a good minister from a bad minister is to test them by their fruit. How well do they stay with God's Word? Are they giving you their version of the Bible or are they giving you the unadulterated Word of God? Test them against God's Word. Are they teaching traditions of men as God's Word? The books of 1st and 2nd Timothy give you excellent guide lines as to how to judge churches and ministers. Paul writes in great detail on the subject.

Can you see the fruits of the Spirit from Galatians 5:22-23 in their Christian walk? Are they prideful? Do they use flattery to control and manipulate people? Psalm 12:2-3 speaks to the subject like this, *"They speak vanity every one with his neighbour; with flattering lips and with a double heart do they speak. The LORD shall cut off all flattering lips, and the tongue that speaketh proud things."* Listen well to the words that your minister speaks; see how they compare to what Holy Scripture says.

If you have questions, respectfully ask your minister to show you in God's Word where what he taught is validated. If he is Biblically sound then he can back everything up that he has preached in the Word of God. He should welcome your questions because it shows that you are studying God's Word, he should never be angry that you have questions. If he is not able to show you chapter and verse, precept upon precept, line upon line, verse upon verse (Isaiah 28:10) where he taught from then you need to rethink if this is really the church that you should be in.

Go to God in prayer and let God be your guide. Seek God's Wisdom on the subject. Matthew 7:20-23 declares for us, *"Wherefore by their fruits ye shall know them. Not everyone that saith unto me, LORD, LORD, shall enter into the kingdom of heaven: but he that doeth the Will of my Father which is in heaven. Many will say to me in that day LORD, LORD, have we not prophesied in thy name? And in thy name have cast out devils? And in thy name done many wonderful works? And then will I profess unto them, I never knew you: depart from me, ye that work iniquity."*

CHAPTER 51

HOW DO WE PRAY TO GOD WHEN WE HAVE REALLY SCREWED UP?

There are times in all of our lives when we really screw up. No way around it, we couldn't have done a better job at messing up our life if we had been given directions to follow. So how do we go about setting things right when we have caused them to be so wrong? Before I speak to the subject I would like to reacquaint you with the story of King David. Most of you will remember him from the Old Testament and if you don't, you should.

We first see David as a youth tending the sheep from his father's flocks. At this time King Saul had just disobeyed God by not following His instructions given in 1st Samuel 15:3, *"Now go and smite Amalek, and utterly destroy all that they have, and spare them not; but slay both man and woman, infant and suckling, ox and sheep, camel and ass."*

A side note here: this is where the movie *"One Night with the King"* starts, which is an excellent family movie. Saul left the king and the queen alive and the best of the live stock. God viewed this act of disobedience as evil on the part of King Saul; King Saul tried to justify leaving the animals alive for a sacrifice to God.

The Prophet Samuel was rebuking King Saul for his disobedience to God. He said to King Saul in 1st Samuel 15:22-23, *"And Samuel said, Hath the LORD as great delight in burnt offerings and sacrifices, as in obeying the voice of the LORD? Behold, to obey is better than sacrifice, and to hearken than the fat of rams. For rebellion is as the sin of witchcraft, and stubbornness is as iniquity and idolatry. Because thou hast rejected the Word of the LORD, He hath also rejected thee from being king."*

God took the office of king from Saul and directed the Prophet Samuel to go and anoint a new king from the sons of Jesse, the Bethlehemite

(1st Samuel 16:1). Samuel obeyed God and after passing over David's seven older brothers God told him to anoint the youngest David as the king of all Israel. God explained to Samuel that the outer appearance (most probably because of David's youth and stature) was not important to God but what was in a man's heart (1st Samuel 16:7).

Now King Saul was not aware that David was the anointed new king, and as the Spirit of the LORD descended upon David it left King Saul. During this time King Saul had a troubled spirit and he asked one of his servants to find him a man who could play music on the harp to soothe him; and one of the servants of Saul recommended David. David was able to quiet the evil spirits that tormented Saul by playing the harp; and over time Saul loved David to the point that he made him his armour bearer.

Most people are familiar with the story of David and Goliath. What you may not be so familiar with is that after the Prophet Samuel had anointed David and the Spirit of God had descended upon David he had killed a lion and a bear protecting his father's sheep. So when David heard that an uncircumcised Philistine was defying the armies of the living God he took offense and the boldness that God had put in his heart arose to the surface once again.

The giant Goliath was insulted when he saw a youth stand in front of him to do battle with him. We see his reaction to David in 1st Samuel 17:43-44, *"And the Philistine said to David, Am I a dog that thou comest to me with staves? And the Philistine cursed David by his gods…Come to me, and I will give thy flesh unto the fowls of the air, and to the beasts of the field."*

David's response to the giant was incredibly bold with the Spirit of God. Remember, that David is considered by many Biblical historians to have been around 15 or 16 years of age, red-haired and with a ruddy complexion, and not too tall where as Goliath is considered to be about nine feet tall. The story continues in 1st Samuel chapter 17:45-47, *"Then said David to the Philistine, Thou comest to me with a sword, and with a spear, and with a shield: but I come to thee in the Name of the LORD of Hosts, the God of the armies of Israel, whom thou hast defied. This day will the LORD deliver thee into mine hand; and I will smite thee, and take thine head from thee; and I will give the carcases of the host of the Philistines this day unto the fowls of the air, and to the wild beasts of the earth; that all the earth may know that there is a God in Israel. And all this assembly shall know that the LORD saveth not with sword and spear: for the battle is the LORD'S, and He will give you into our hands."*

You should know the rest of the story; David slew Goliath with a stone from his slingshot that landed in the forehead of the giant and killed him. Possibly you may not know this but David's choosing "five" smooth stones is indicative of God's Grace upon him. The number five in Biblical Numeric's means grace. This is a very interesting subject on its own, and if you would like to do a deeper study I highly recommend the book "*Biblical Mathematics, Keys to Scripture Numeric's, How to Count the Bible*", by Ed F. Vallowe. This book will give you an in depth study of how well God has planned every little detail in the Bible even down to each and every time a specific number was used in Scripture. It will amaze you.

Saul became very jealous of David even though he did love him. Part of this jealousy was fueled because the women of the town would sing a song that honored David for slaying his ten thousands, while they praised King Saul for only killing thousands (1st Samuel 18:7). Saul would go back and forth with David, sometimes being very kind to him and giving him much honor, even to the point of letting his youngest daughter marry David, while other times he would directly try to kill him.

All throughout this time while David was on the run for his life he still showed respect and love to King Saul. Eventually King Saul was wounded in battle with the Philistines and rather than be captured and abused by the Philistines, he fell on his sword and died (1st Samuel 31:4). David then became the official King of Israel.

David was a good king but he was far from being perfect. While he was king he angered God several times and punishment did follow. The reason why I am refreshing your memory of David is to show you that even God's anointed can screw up grievously. King David lusted (2nd Samuel 11:2-4) after the wife of one of his mighty men named Uriah. Bathsheba conceived a child with David, David tried to get her husband to come home from battle to sleep with her, so as to cover his sin. The Book of Luke in chapter 12 verse 2 speaks to this: *"For there is nothing covered, that shall not be revealed; neither hid, that shall not be known."* Uriah was an honorable man and told David: "How can I sleep in the comforts of my home, when my men are on the battlefield and are sleeping in the open fields?"

Nothing David could do, even getting Uriah drunk could convince him to sleep with his wife and in his house. So David had Uriah take a letter from him to Joab (David's nephew and one of his captains in charge of the battle) that said to put Uriah in the fore front of the hottest battle. This insured that Uriah would die and that King David could marry Bathsheba. 2nd Samuel 11:27 continues the story of David, *"And when the mourning was past, David sent and fetched her to his house, and she became his wife, and bare him a son. But the thing that David had done displeased the LORD."*

The LORD sent the Prophet Nathan to speak His judgment upon the house of David for his vile acts against God's Laws. The story again continues in 2nd Samuel 12:10-16, *"Now therefore the sword shall never depart from thine house; because thou hast despised me, and hast taken the wife of Uriah the Hittite to be thy wife. Thus saith the LORD, Behold, I will raise up evil against thee out of thine own house, and I will take thy wives before thine eyes, and give them unto thy neighbour, and he shall lie with thy wives in the sight of this sun. For thou didst it secretly: but I will do this thing before all Israel, and before the sun.*

And David said unto Nathan, I have sinned against the LORD. And Nathan said unto David, The LORD also hath put away thy sin; thou shalt not die. Howbeit, because by this deed thou hast given great occasion to the enemies of the LORD to blaspheme, the child also that is born unto thee shall surely die. And Nathan departed unto his house. And the LORD struck the child that Uriah's wife bare unto David, and it was very sick. David therefore besought God for the child; and David fasted, and went in, and lay all night upon the earth. And the elders of his house arose, and went to him, to raise him up from the earth: but he would not, neither did he eat bread with them. And it came to pass on the seventh day, that the child died..."

God takes disobedience by His children very seriously. David's punishment lasted until the day he died. His children never provided him a moment of peace throughout his life time. David's son Amnon raped his half sister Tamar, which in turn disgraced her for the rest of her life. After waiting two years her brother Absalom killed Amnon to get revenge for the rape of his sister. After Amnon's death, Absalom was in exile three years before he was able to return to Jerusalem and even then it was a full two years more before King David would chose to see him.

Absalom was considered to be a very handsome man and also a very prideful man. Once he was back in the king's good graces, he set about to undermine David's authority and respect in any way that he could and by doing this he stole the hearts of the men of Israel (2nd Samuel 15:6).

Forty years later Absalom declared war on his father to take the kingship away from him. He was eventually defeated by David and Absalom met a gruesome and an untimely death. Absalom had extremely long and thick hair and when he realized that he was defeated by his father he rode through the woods to escape being captured by his father's men. The mule that he was riding on went under the low hanging branches of an oak tree, the branches snagged him up by his hair and left him hanging in the air. Joab heard about it and went and quickly executed him.

Even when David was very old and near death chaos still reigned in his family. He had promised the throne to his son Solomon and when he was on his death bed his son Adonijah declared himself to be king and even started celebrating with music, food and drink. David had the Prophet Nathan and the Priest Zadok officially anoint Solomon the king to succeed him. When Adonijah and the people who were celebrating with him, heard that Solomon was the legal king they hid fearing that Solomon would punish them and even Adonijah begged mercy of his younger brother. God forgave David of all of his sins, but God also, in his justice, let David live with the punishment and consequences of his disobedience.

There is nothing so bad that you could have done in this life, even if you have committed murder, that will preclude you from God's forgiveness. He will forgive you just as he forgave David, but you will have to live with the consequences of your actions. Every time that David disobeyed God, he would come to his senses and be truly repentant of his sins. He would come before God with a contrite and a broken spirit.

On the next page, I have included Psalm 51. Read this Psalm slowly and thoughtfully. Keep in mind that David wrote this Psalm to God to express how deep his grief was over his sins of disobedience and the knowledge that he had deeply offended God. This was right after David had spent a week prostate on the ground praying to God for forgiveness and the life of his son. David's grief at the separation that his sin had caused between him and God was real and heartfelt.

All of the verses are good but look and consider especially verses 10-12. They are, *"Create in me a clean heart, O God; and renew a right spirit within me. Cast me not away from thy presence: and take not thy Holy Spirit from me. Restore unto me the joy of thy salvation; and uphold me with thy free spirit."* I don't think that, in the Bible, there is a better example of a sinner whose heart is truly convicted with the realization and pain of his sin. Never think that you can't come before God and ask forgiveness for what you have done. If you are having trouble finding the right words, feel free to use David's. I don't think you will find words more perfectly or sincerely stated.

PSALM 51

Have mercy upon me,
O God,
According to thy loving-kindness:
According unto the multitude
Of thy tender mercies
Blot out my transgression.

Wash me thoroughly from mine iniquity,
And cleanse me from my sin.
For I acknowledge
My transgressions:
And my sin is ever before me
Against thee,
Thee only,
Have I sinned,
And done this evil
In thy sight;
That thou mightest be justified
When thou speakest,
And be clear when thou judgest.

Behold,
Thou desirest truth
In the inward parts:
And in the hidden part
Thou shalt make me
To know wisdom.

Purge me with hyssop*,
And I shall be clean:

---

*Hyssop is nowadays called Oregano, it is considered by many to have an antibiotic effect on the body. Wild oregano from the Mediterranean is sold in health food stores as oil or a capsule

*Wash me,
And I shall be whiter
Than snow.*

*Make me to hear
Joy and gladness;
That the bones
Which thou hast broken
May rejoice.*

*Hide thy face
From my sins,
And blot out
All mine iniquities.*

*Create in me
A clean heart,
O God;
And renew a right spirit
Within me
Cast me not
Away from thy presence;
And take not thy Holy Spirit from me.*

*Restore
Unto me
The joy
Of thy salvation;
And uphold
Me with thy free spirit.*

*Then will I teach
Transgressors thy ways;
And sinners
Shall be converted unto thee.*

Deliver me
From blood guiltiness*,
O God,
Thou God of my salvation:
And my tongue
Shall sing aloud
Of thy righteousness.

O LORD,
Open thou my lips:
And my mouth
Shall show forth thy praise

For thou desirest not sacrifice;
Else would I give it:
Thou delightest not in burnt offering.

The sacrifices of God
Are a broken spirit:
A broken and a contrite heart,
O God,
Thou wilt not despise.

Do good
In thy good pleasure unto Zion:
Build thou the walls of Jerusalem.

Then shalt thou be pleased
With the sacrifices of righteousness,
With burnt offering
And whole burnt offering:

---

*Blood guiltiness meaning "blood as that which, when shed, causes death". This most likely is in reference here to Uriah.

Then
Shall they
Offer bullocks upon thine altar.

Don't ever think that because you have sinned that you are useless to God's purposes. Even David with all of his failing was still used by God to His Glory. The blood line of Jesus Christ runs through David and his family. We all fall short of the Glory of God (Romans 3:23), but it is by His unmerited mercy and grace to us that He will forgive us of all of our sins and offer us the gift of His Salvation. There is nothing that we can do to earn our salvation; it is a gift from God, freely given to us His children because He loves us. Ephesians 2:8-9 says it clearly for us, *"For by grace are ye saved through faith: and that not of yourselves: it is the gift of God: Not of works, lest any man should boast."*

CHAPTER 52

DON'T WORRY BE HAPPY (COUNT IT ALL JOY)

"Don't Worry, Be Happy", is the title from a hit song in 1988 by Bobby McFerrin. You just have to look at Philippians 4:4-7 to see that the Word of God agrees with this song, *"Rejoice in the LORD always: and again I say, rejoice. Let your moderation be known unto all men. The LORD is at hand. Be careful for nothing* (meaning - don't be anxious about anything)*; but in everything by prayer and supplication with thanksgiving let your requests be made known unto God. And the peace of God, which passeth all understanding, shall keep your hearts and minds though Christ Jesus."*

Hebrews 11:6 speaks to us this way, *"But without faith it is impossible to please Him: for he that cometh to God must believe that He is, and that He is a rewarder of them that diligently seek Him."* Concern for a person or a situation is good but when concern is perverted by the devil it becomes worry. When we worry or fret over a given situation then we doubt that God can take care of the situation.

Dr. Lester Sumrall, in his book, *'Take It...It's Yours, Seizing Your Spiritual Dominion"*, expresses it this way:

> The devil is an expert in guerilla warfare. He sneaks in unaware, coming in camouflage. He is a deceiver, using deception to create fears, phobias, confusion, and feelings of helplessness. Man receives these terrible things, not because the devil cannot be overcome but because man listens to the devil's voice.[17]

Fear or worry is not trusting God to take care of us and to protect us. Fear or worry is the absence of faith in our hearts. Deuteronomy 31:6 says it like this, *"Be strong and of a good courage, fear not, nor be*

---

[17] Sumrall, Lester, Take *It... It's Yours, Seizing Your Spiritual Dominion* (South Bend, Indiana: Lester Sumrall Evangelistic Association, 1986), p. 40.

afraid of them: for the LORD thy God, He it is that doth go with thee: He will not fail thee, nor forsake thee." There are at least 62 scriptures that say "Fear Not" in them and there are additional ones that speak of having no fear but just say it a little bit differently. Holy Scripture makes it very clear that we are to put our faith and trust in the LORD and to give Him our cares. Isaiah 35:4 further states to us, *"Say to them that are of a fearful heart, be strong, fear not: behold, your God will come with vengeance, even God with a recompence: He will come and save you."*

Fear can paralyze us from living our lives to the fullest. Fear and any other negative emotion can keep us locked in both emotional and physical bondage. John 8:36 teaches us, *"If the Son therefore shall make you free, ye shall be free indeed."* God is the only one who can break the bondages that keep us in our own personal jail. Psalm 34:4 says to us, *"I sought the LORD, and He heard me, and delivered me from all my fears."* We have to come to Him in prayer to ask Him do this for us, but the freedom that He offers us is very real. Galatians 5:1 speaks to the subject of bondage like this, *"Stand fast therefore in the liberty wherewith Christ hath made us free, and be not entangled again with the yoke of bondage."*

Dr. Sumrall continues by giving us a better understanding of the importance of prayer in overcoming our fears and worries:

> Prayer is the key that unlocks the treasures of God.
> Prayer is power…
> The act of praying generates omnipotence. Prayer gives the frail human reed unshakeable strength.
> If you do not know how to pray, you do not know the power of God. Prayer is the most talked about, discussed, and the least used power available to mankind.
> Oil, undiscovered, is an untapped resource. Coal, not mined, is an untapped source of power. But the greatest source of untapped power and resource is prayer. All that prayer can do has never

yet been defined. This tremendous source of power has never been fully researched or developed.[18]

Nowadays I love to travel with my husband, but there was a time in my life before I had a personal relationship with God that I hated the idea of traveling, I only felt safe at home. I didn't like the loud traffic noises and all of the cars going so fast on the freeways really scared me. I even went so far as to bring a magazine or a book to look at if I knew we would be in heavy freeway traffic. It just panicked me to see all of the cars speeding by and it gave me a sense of being out of control. I didn't like sleeping in hotels and I found it hard to find food that agreed with me while on the road.

Looking back on it now I know that it was fear that held me in bondage and was keeping me from enjoying all of the new things and experiences that you have when traveling. Though at the time I could not see that my thinking was rooted in fear; it was just other people who couldn't understand my logic. If God had not set me free from my illogical fear, I never would have experienced all of the wonderful places, people and new experiences that I have come to love. Now I eagerly look forward to our next excursion.

Because God has broken the shackles of fear off of me I have been able to enjoy such things as catching a cat nap under a brightly lit and flashing marquee in Primm, Nevada; seeing smog and palm trees first hand in California; in the western states stars so breathtakingly beautiful that it looks like you could reach out and touch them with your hands; tumble weeds blowing across the highway out west in a sudden rain storm; Prairie Dogs begging for scraps at rest stops; Love bugs in Louisiana; all 480 miles of the Natchez Trace (and at night it gets kind of creepy); in the shadows of night time, a tree that looks like a T-Rex charging you at a rest stop in Maine and the magnificent strength and beauty of Niagara Falls.

---

[18] Sumrall, p. 70-71.

I can't leave this subject without speaking to how much fun it is to stop at a Flying J rest stop and gas station. They seem to have some of the best choices for meals on the highway and also a very eclectic selection of wares to buy. These are just a few of the places and sights that God's unmerited grace and mercy have allowed me to enjoy. 2nd Corinthians 3:17 says that where the Spirit of the LORD is there is liberty. Finally in Psalm 119:45 Holy Scripture declares to us, *"And I will walk at liberty: for I seek thy precepts."*

CHAPTER 53

"Write the vision", HABAKKUK 2:2

"And the LORD answered me, and said, Write the vision, and make it plain upon tables..." God's Word declares for us that we are to write down on paper what we want God to do in our lives. Once again don't ask to be the best bank robber; your vision needs to be within the boundaries of God's Commandments which means His Will for us. Be specific in what you want from God. This is all part of the authority that our Father God has given us in Romans 4:17, *"...calleth those things which be not as though they were."*

1st John 5:14 states for us that *"And this is the confidence that we have in Him, that if we ask any thing according to His Will, He heareth us: And if we know that He hear us, whatsoever we ask, we know that we have the petitions that we desired of Him."* Job 22:28 continues the thought with, *"Thou shalt also decree a thing, and it shall be established unto thee: and the light shall shine upon thy ways."* John 15:7 declares, *"If ye abide in me, and my words abide in you, ye shall ask what ye will, and it shall be done unto you."* Finally in 1st John 3:22 His Word says, *"And whatsoever we ask, we receive of Him, because we keep His commandments, and do those things that are pleasing in His sight."*

Proverbs 18:21 declares to us that *"Death and life are in the power of the tongue..."* Our words have the power of life and death in them. This is why you find in Psalm 39:1 that Scripture teaches us to bridle your tongue so that you will not sin. Be very careful with the words that come out of your mouth. The old childhood adage that says *"sticks and stones may break my bones but words will never hurt me"* is not true.

Words can pierce right to your heart. Hurtful words can stay with us a lifetime and often times those same hurtful words will shape who we become. We subconsciously walk in bondage to those hurtful words as much as if we dragged a ball and chain upon our ankle. Kind and loving words will impact a person for life too. Choose wisely the words that you speak into people's lives including your own. They become a legacy for blessings from God or cursings from God.

When you look at what Scripture declares about us as believers in Christ you see all that we can be in Christ. Take time to truly study Deuteronomy 28:1-14; you will see what God promises to us if and when we walk in obedience to His commandments. These promises are called a "Profession of Faith" because this is who we are when we are followers of Christ. Here are some of them. We will be blessed in our life, our children will be blessed, and everything that we put our hands to will be blessed. We will be blessed when we come in and when we go out. The LORD will take care of your enemies. We are the lender, not the borrower. We are the head, not the tail; and we are above, not beneath.

Now read and carefully study the rest of Deuteronomy 28 to see what God promises to those who choose to walk in disobedience to His commandments. It is our free will choice to choose cursings or blessings. Deuteronomy 11:26-28 states it very clearly for us, *"Behold, I set before you this day a blessing and a curse; A blessing, if ye obey the commandments of the LORD your God, which I command you this day: And a curse, if ye will not obey the commandments of the LORD your God, but turn aside out of the way which I command you this day, to go after other gods, which ye have not known"*

You can pray these promises as your profession of faith to God. This would be calling those things that are not, as if they are and then they will be (Romans 4:17). In the 2nd book of Kings Chapter 4 we see the story of a Shunammite women's profession of faith. She and her husband were childless and unlike today, in Biblical times it was a disgrace to be barren. She was a woman of some importance and she and her husband provided a private room for the Prophet Elisha to stay in when he was in their area. After a while the Prophet Elisha asked her how he could properly thank her for the kindness that she and her husband had shown him and his servant. She responded that she was not in need of anything. His servant pointed out that she was childless and in about a year's time she had a son.

Well the child grew and one day he was out in the fields with his father and became very ill. The father sent him back to be cared for by his mother. In a matter of time, the child died. She then placed him on the bed that she had for the Prophet Elisha as if he was just sleeping. She told her husband that all was well but that she wanted to go to see the Prophet. She quickly went to the town where he was and caught him by his feet. He knew that something was seriously wrong. She told him to remember that when he had declared that she would have a child that she had said to him not to deceive her. He sent his servant to heal the child but the servant was unsuccessful. The Prophet then went to the woman's house and performed a miracle and restored her son to life.

What is so wonderful about this story is that all throughout this ordeal of her son dying, the woman never gave up her belief that somehow God would restore her son to life and that all would be well with her. Her Profession of Faith in God was "all is well in my life." She said this to her husband fully knowing that her son was dead. She guarded her tongue so that only words of life came out of her mouth. We need to declare this same profession of faith over all areas of our life too. We need to pray that in the Name of Jesus Christ we declare that all is well in our lives every day.

Now if you go back to Deuteronomy 28:1-14 you'll find additional blessings to confess that you believe and that you receive them from God. For example, you could say that I am the head not the tail; I am the lender not the borrower and so on. You can also add to your Profession of Faith that you are blessed with the favor of God, that you are accepted, and that you are free from condemnation. You can also confess over your life the blessings of God's unbounded mercy and grace towards you, God's unconditional love for you and that you are blessed when you come in and blessed when you go out.

When you are praying like this you can also personalize your Profession of Faith, possibly something like this; *"I confess, believe and receive from God that all is well in my life. As long as the promises of God stay the same then my profession of faith will stay the same, all is well in my life. I confess, believe and receive from God that all of our debts are demolished, that our children are excellent students in school, that I am healed by His stripes, and that all that I put my hands to is blessed by God."* It will take a little bit of forethought and practice but this profession of faith in God that all is well in my life should be something that we profess every day.

Don't limit your profession of faith to Deuteronomy 28:1-14. There are lots of places from scripture to take additional statements from to include in your Confession of Faith. God speaks loudly as to whom we are when we are walking in Him. The more that you profess who you are in God, and who God says you are, the more that you will begin to reflect God in your words and actions.

Dr. Lester Sumrall, in his book *Take It...It's Yours, Seizing Your Spiritual Dominion,* teaches us about the power of your confession of faith this way:

> An age-long strategy of the devil is to attack the believer in the area of confession. He knows a person will never rise above his confession. Instead of making the promises of God his confession of faith, the believer constantly confesses his sickness, faults, and weaknesses. Since a man is what he confesses himself to be, the devil uses this means to keep the believer in bondage.
> Satan does not want you to confess your position of dominion in Christ or your victories by the Blood of God's Son. When you make these your confession, you exert dominion, authority, and power.[19]

---

[19] Sumrall, Lester, *Take It...It's Yours, Seizing Your Spiritual Dominion* (South Bend, Indiana: Lester Sumrall Evangelistic Association, 1986), p. 56.

CHAPTER 54

WHAT DOES GOD SAY ABOUT FASTING?

Fasting is another area that you may not be aware that God speaks on. In Matthew 6:16 God says *when* you fast, not "if". So fasting is one of those things like prayer that God has very definite ideas on for us. I am not going to go into all of the safe rules for fasting here but I would highly recommend that you read *"If My People, a guide on Fasting and Prayer"* by Sun Fannin with Larry Fannin. What I do want to point out to you is that fasting is for our benefit so that we can better focus on God and what He has to say to us.

I know a lot of people will have the response "well, I just can't go without food or water for any length of time." You might be surprised to learn that while your body will die without water, it can survive without food for quite a while.

There are different types of food fasts that the above book will go into detail on so that you can proceed with your fast safely. After reading this book if you are unsure if fasting is medically safe for you check, with your doctor. God does not want you to do anything that is going to endanger your health and your doctor will be able to guide you if there might be a problem with medications or physical fasting for you.

Also, you do need to know that if you are for whatever reason not able to do a food fast then there are additional ways to fast. You can fast a favorite T.V. show (or maybe T.V. for a day or longer), soda pop, candy and the list goes on. It doesn't have to be food; it can be an activity that you love. You might for example ask God to help you do a fast by using baby steps. So maybe you start by putting off your lunch time an extra fifteen minutes. Or maybe you just try fasting on Monday's. Either way fasting is something that we should do as we can, it spiritually cleans out the trash in us, and it will enhance your relationship with God and bring you closer to Him.

When you are fasting you will want to pray more also. Jesus spoke to the Twelve Disciples in chapter 17:14-21 of the book of Matthew. The Twelve had been unable to cast out the devil from a man's son and didn't understand why they had failed. *"And Jesus said unto them, Because of your unbelief: for verily I say unto you, If ye have faith as a grain of mustard seed, ye shall say unto this mountain, Remove hence to yonder place and it shall remove; and nothing shall be impossible unto you. Howbeit this kind goeth not out but by prayer and fasting"* Matthew 17:20-21. When you are struggling with a long term problem, fasting and prayer can break the strongholds that are keeping you from being successful. Our not being obedient to God, by not fasting, can also be a blessing blocker.

CHAPTER 55

TITHING...DID I SAY *TITHING*?

Everything that we have in this life is from our Father God. Every breath we take; every beautiful sight that we see; everything that we feel with our sense of touch, every smell, every taste, and every sound we hear and each and every beat of our heart comes from a loving and a gracious God. Everything that we have is from God because He loves us and wants us to live life to its fullest. John 10:10 declares for us that, *"... I am come that they might have life, and that they might have it more abundantly."*

That said though most people don't understand the Biblical principle of tithing. Because God has given us everything we have it is only right that we give back 10% to Him. God's Holy Word teaches us about tithing this way in Malachi 3:8-10, *"Will a man rob God? Yet ye have robbed me. But ye say, Wherein have we robbed thee? In tithes and offerings. Ye are cursed with a curse: for ye have robbed me, even this whole nation. Bring ye all the tithes into the storehouse, that there may be meat in mine house, and prove me now herewith, saith the LORD of Hosts, if I will not open you the windows of heaven, and pour you out a blessing, that there shall not be room enough to receive it."*

God doesn't need our tithe, but if you don't give back to Him to acknowledge that He is our Jehovah-Jireh, then you are not walking in obedience to Him and you will be blocking your blessings from God. You don't have to tithe, God will not force you to tithe but if you choose not to tithe then don't expect God to bless you. Luke 6:38 confirms it for us this way, *"Give, and it shall be given unto you; good measure, pressed down, and shaken together, and running over, shall men give into your bosom. For with the same measure that ye mete withal it shall be measured to you again."*

You cannot out give God, when you tithe freely then God will bless you and your family with more than enough for your needs and your wants and also enough so that you can bless others. We don't follow a God of barely enough; we follow a God whose blessings upon us will fill up and spill over our largest cup.

Some people will use the excuse that they don't tithe because they feel that the money that they give to church only goes to the minister and in their thinking ministers should live in constant poverty. You need to realize that this idea for our ministers to be poverty stricken comes from a denominational thinking that is not rooted in the Word of God. Somehow the idea of a minister being poverty stricken has been confused with the notion that the poorer they are the holier that they will be. This is not true, and it comes from a tradition of men. Dr. Lester Sumrall speaks to the dangers of blindly following traditions of men in his book *Take It…It's Yours, Seizing Your Spiritual Dominion*.

> Tradition is a terrible, destructive influence that can bury you. You can get so steeped in tradition that you say, "It's always been done that way, and we are always going to do it that way." If you are bound by tradition, God cannot move in your life in a new way to help and bless you.[20]

God wants all of His people to walk in the fullness of His blessings. When we are walking in submission and obedience to God then God wants us to have His best and His best does not mean poverty or a near poverty life style of His shepherds or His sheep. Luke 10:7 and Matthew 10:10 both speak of a servant being worthy of his hire which means pay God's servants a fair wage. A fair wage does not mean poverty.

A minister of God should be the first person to try to help people with their problems. If the minister of God barely has enough money to put food on his table and buy clothes for his family, then he is not in a

---

[20] Sumrall, Lester, *Take It…It's Yours, Seizing Your Spiritual Dominion* (South Bend, Indiana: Lester Sumrall Evangelistic Association, 1986), p. 90.

position to bless others because he is not being blessed. If a church is being properly run then the minister does not have the authority to set his own pay, it should be done by a Church Board of Directors. So the theory that the minister is going to be running away with the church offerings does not hold water in a church that is run by God's rules, not man's.

One additional thought on the subject of tithing. If you can't give your tithe to God freely and with a cheerful heart then God does not want it. Like love that is coerced, a tithe that is given begrudgingly has no value to God. Any offering that you give to God that is not of your own free will is not wanted by God. 2nd Corinthians 9:6-8 states it this way: *"But this I say, He which soweth sparingly shall reap also sparingly; and he which soweth bountifully shall reap also bountifully. Every man according as he purposeth in his heart, so let him give: not grudgingly, or of necessity: for God loveth a cheerful giver. And God is able to make all grace abound toward you; that ye, always having all sufficiency in all things, may abound to every good work."*

A tithe is not just limited to your money. You can tithe your time and or abilities. Proverbs 3:9-10 says it this way, *"Honour the LORD with thy substance, and with the first fruits of all thine increase: So shall thy barns be filled with plenty, and thy presses shall burst out with new wine."*

CHAPTER 56

"...For I will never leave thee, nor forsake thee" **Hebrews 13:5**

Who is God? Holy Scripture tells us that God is three distinct and equal persons in one, The Father, The Son and the Holy Ghost or Spirit. This is the mystery of the Trinity and it is one mystery that until we stand before God we will not have the full understanding of it. What does Scripture say about the names of God? *"And thou shall call His name JESUS"* (Matthew 1:21); *"Wonderful, Counselor, The Mighty God, The Everlasting Father, The Prince of Peace"* (Isaiah 9:6); *"Holy One"* (Mark 1:24); *"The Lamb of God which taketh away the sin of the world"* (John 1:29); *"Prince of Life"* (Acts 3:15); *"LORD God Almighty"* (Revelation 3:15); *"Lion of the Tribe of Judah, Root of David"* (Revelation 5:5); *"Word of Life"* (1st John 1:1); *"Author and Finisher of our Faith"* (Hebrews 12:2); *"Advocate"* (1st John 2:1); *"The Way, The Truth, and the Life"* (John 14:6); *"Dayspring from on high"* (Luke 1:78); *"LORD of All"* (Acts 10:36); *"I am"* (John 8:58); *"Son of God"* (John 1:34); *"Shepherd and Bishop of Souls"* (1st Peter 2:25); *"Messiah...the Christ"* (John 1:41); *"The Lord and Savior Jesus Christ"* (2nd Peter 2:20); *"Chief Cornerstone"* (Ephesians 2:20); *"KING OF KINGS, AND LORD OF LORDS"* (Revelation 19:16); *"Righteous Judge"* (2nd Timothy 4:8); *"Light of the World"* (John 8:12); *"Head of the Church"* (Ephesians 1:22); *"The Root and the Offspring of David, and the Bright and Morning Star"* (Revelation 22:16); *"Sun of Righteousness"* (Malachi 4:2); *"LORD Jesus Christ"* (Acts 15:11); *"Chief Shepherd"* (1st Peter 5:4); *"Resurrection and Life"* (John 11:25); *"Horn of Salvation"* (Luke 1: 69); *"Governor"* (Matthew 2:6); and finally *"The Alpha and The Omega"* (Revelation 1:8).

How does this apply to us? It applies to us because Scripture tells us that as believers we are saved forever by grace through faith (Ephesians 2:8). As believers we are justified by faith and we are at peace with God through our LORD Jesus Christ (Romans 5:1). As believers, we are *"Forgiven"* (Ephesians 1:7); *"Beloved of God"* (Romans 1:7);

"Servants of the Most High God" (Acts 16:17); *"A New Creature"* (2nd Corinthians 5:17); *"Dead to Sin and Alive to God"* (Romans 6:1); *"Walking in the Newness of Life"* (Romans 6:4); *"Baptized into Christ Jesus"* (Romans 6:3); *"The Temple of the Holy Spirit"* (1st Corinthians 6:19-20); *"Clothed with Christ"* (Galatians 3:27); *"Holy"* (Hebrews 3:1); *"Blameless"* (1st Corinthians 1:8); *"Victorious"* (1st Corinthians 15:57); *"Ministers of Reconciliation"* (2nd Corinthians 5:18); *"Fishers of Men"* (Mark 1:17); *"One in Christ"* (Galatians 3:28); *"Salt of the Earth"* (Matthew 5:13); *"Children of Promise"* (Galatians 4:28); *"Light of the World"* (Matthew 5:14); *"Seated in Heaven"* (Ephesians 2:6); *"A Good Soldier of Jesus Christ"* (2nd Timothy 2:3); *"Christians"* (Acts 11:26); *"You Are Born Again"* (1st Peter 1:23); *"And the Body of Christ"* (1st Corinthians 12:27).

Who are we in Jesus Christ? Psalm 4:3 tells us, *"But know that the LORD hath set apart him that is godly for Himself; the LORD will hear when I call unto Him."* Know that your choice to walk with God sets you apart from the world, we are told to be in the world not of the world (John 15:19). Fully realize here that your choice to have a personal relationship with God will set you at odds with the morally bankrupt culture of today. You will pay a price in this world for your relationship with God. Expect that people may ridicule you because you do not walk in lock step with what our society today says is okay and modern.

Matthew 5:13-14 tells us that we are to be the salt of the earth and the light of the world. We are the difference makers. We are not just to be the followers we are to be the leaders. We are to set the tone and the example for others. Who are we in Jesus Christ? We are forgiven (Ephesians 1:7), we are accepted in Christ (1st John 3:1), and we are beloved of God (Romans 1:7). 1st Corinthians 6:19-20 teaches us, *"What? Know ye not that your body is the temple of the Holy Ghost which is in you, which ye have of God, and ye are not your own? For ye are bought with a price: therefore glorify God in your body, and in your spirit which are God's."* We are the Body of Christ (1st Corinthians 12:27), we are children of promise (Galatians 4:28), we are seated in heaven (Ephesians 2:6) and finally in Ephesians 2:10, *"For we are His workmanship, created in Christ Jesus unto good works, which God hath before ordained that we should walk in them."*

Why is all of this so very important to us? It is not just important to you it is critical to you to know who you are in Christ and whose you are. Who are you in Christ Jesus? Scripture tells us that we are a child of God (John 1:12); we are a *"friend"* of God (John 15:15); we have been *"justified in Christ"* (Romans 5:1); *"we are an adopted child of God"* (Ephesians 1:5); *"In whom we have redemption through His blood, even the forgiveness of sins"* (Colossians 1:14); We cannot be separated from the love of Christ (Romans 8:35); *"And you are complete in Him..."* (Colossians 2:10). This is just some of what Holy Scripture tells us that our identity is as a believer in God.

If you never know who you are in Christ, then you will forever walk in ignorance as to your true identity and to your true inheritance as a child of the Most High God. Hosea 4:6 teaches us that my people perish for lack of knowledge. Additionally you will forever walk in ignorance to the power and authority that you have in the Name of Jesus Christ and the Blood of Christ if you never learn whose child you are. Luke 10:19-20 says it like this, *"Behold, I give unto you power* (meaning authority) *to tread on serpents and scorpions, and over all the power of the enemy: and nothing shall by any means hurt you. Notwithstanding in this rejoice not, that the spirits* (the supernatural) *are subject unto you: but rather rejoice, because your names are written in heaven."*

The circle is complete, I once again ask you, why pray? You should pray to have a deep and an intimate relationship with God so that you will know Him as your "Abba Father." You should pray so that you walk in the fullest of knowledge of God so that you are secure in who you are in Christ Jesus. You should pray so that you are rock solid sure that you know that God will never leave you nor forsake you. The Name of Jesus should be what is on your lips more than any other name. It should be the first name that you call out in times of troubles and blessings.

It's possible that you may be thinking "well how can I get to that level of intimacy and security in God?" Once again, I will answer you, with baby steps. All of this transformation does not just happen overnight. It takes a concentrated effort on your part. So what do I mean by baby steps here, especially keeping in mind how busy your day is? You possibly start by praying when you're showering, driving, doing dishes, walking the dog and or doing laundry. Any small amount of time that you give to God, He will honor it. Don't forget to sing to our Father God, He loves to hear your voice. Even if you just have time to say "Thank You God for my life, my spouse, my children, my dinner, finding a good parking space or a good sale price, but say thank you because it all comes from Him.

You don't have to set aside an hour or two to make your prayers have value and worth to God. Scripture declares that we despise not small beginning (Zechariah 4:10) so just pick a place and start on your prayer journey. As you honor God with the time that you can give to Him in prayer you will start to automatically pray more often and longer. Something else will begin to happen to you, you will start to hear from God, you will start to recognize His voice and you will more and more enjoy your time and your relationship with God. Your relationship with God will almost become addictive to you. The more you give of yourself to God, the more that He will pour into you and bless you and your family and the more that you will want of God. He will not let you down. You will develop a hunger for God that only knowing Him intimately will satisfy.

Once you get hooked on God there is no going back to the emptiness that you had before. You won't accept crumbs as a relationship; you will only accept a seven course sit down meal, no more fast food type relationships for you. Hebrews 13:5 declares to us that, *"...I will never leave thee, nor forsake thee"* and in Isaiah 40:8 we are taught that, *"The grass withereth, the flower fadeth: but the Word of our God shall stand for ever."* May you learn to count it all joy, may you prosper and be blessed in your walk with God. May you always hunger for His Word and may that hunger drive you continually into His precious Word to be fed.

2ⁿᵈ CHRONICLES 7:14

*"If my people,
Which are
Called by my Name,
Shall humble
Themselves,
And pray,
And seek my face,
And turn
From their wicked ways;
Then will I
Hear from heaven,
And will forgive
Their sin,
And will
Heal their land."*

PSALM 55:16

"As for me,
I will call upon God;
And the LORD shall save me
Evening,
And morning,
And at noon,
Will I pray,
And cry aloud:
And He
Shall hear my voice."

1st THESSALONIANS 5:17-18

"Pray without ceasing.
In every thing
Give thanks:
For this
Is the
Will of God
In Christ Jesus
Concerning you."

In case you haven't asked Jesus to come into your heart and be your LORD and Savior now is a good time to do so. Say this:

Jesus,
I ask that you
Come into my heart
And be my LORD and Savior.

I thank you Father,
For sending Jesus
To die for me
Upon the cross
So that I too
Could be redeemed
Through the Blood of the Lamb.

I ask for forgiveness of my sins.

You know my strengths and weaknesses
My victories and failures
I thank you
That knowing all that I am
You still love me
Unconditionally
And see value
In this lump of clay.
Amen.

BIBLIOGRAPHY

Barton, David. The American Heritage Series with Historian David Barton, Volumes 1-10. Aledo: www.wallbuilders.com, 2007.

Bennett, Dennis and Rita Bennett. "The Holy Spirit and You", Gainesville, FL: Bridge-Logos Publishers, 1998.

Bowling, Sarah and Marilyn Hickey. Blessing The Next Generation. New York: Faith Words, Hachette Book Group, USA, 2008.

Brim, Billye. The Blood and The Glory. Tulsa, OK: Harrison House, Inc., 1995.

Bullinger, E. W., Dr. The Companion Bible, The Authorized Versions of 1611 with the Structures and Critical, Explanatory, and Suggestive Notes and with 198 Appendixes. Grand Rapids, MI: Kregel Publications, 1909.

Dobson, James, Dr. Love Must Be Tough, New Hope for Marriages in Crisis. Sisters, OR: Multnomah Publishers, Inc., 1996.

Fannin, Larry and Sun Fannin. If My People, A Guide on Fasting and Prayer. Shippensburg, PA: Companion Press, 1992.

Gay, Robert. Silencing The Enemy, Lake Mary: Charisma House, FL: A Strang Company, 1993.

Hammond, Frank and Ida Mae Hammond. Pigs In The Parlor, Kirkwood, MO: Impact Christian Book, Inc., 2004.

MacMillan, John A. The Authority of the Believer, Camp Hill, PA: Wing Spread Publishers, 1981.

Osborn, T. L. Healing The Sick. Tulsa, OK: Harrison House Inc., 1992.

Pentecost, J. Dwight, edited by John Danilson, John. A Study of the Life of Christ, The Words and Works of Jesus Christ, Grand Rapids, MI: Zondervan Publishing House, 1981.

Prince, Derek. Spiritual Warfare, Charlotte, NC: Derek Prince Ministries-International, 1987.

Smith, William, Sir, revived and edited by F. N. Peloubet M.A. Smith's Bible Dictionary, A Dictionary of the Bible. Nashville, TN: Thomas Nelson Publishers, 1998.

Strong, James, L.L.D., S.T.D., with some editorial services provided by: Dr. Stanley Morris and John R. Kohlenberger III. The New Strong's Exhaustive Concordance of the Bible. Nashville, TN: Thomas Nelson, Inc., 1995.

Sumrall, Lester. Take It...It's Yours, Seizing Your Spiritual Dominion. South Bend, IN: Lester Sumrall Evangelistic Association, 1986.

Wagner, C. Peter. Your Spiritual Gifts Can Help Your Church Grow. Ventura, CA: Regal Books, 1994.

Scott, Dr. Dick. Nothing but the Blood of Jesus. Online, 26 May 2008. Available http://www.ptm.org/99PT/MarApr/NothingButBlood.htm.

All scripture quotations, unless otherwise noted, are taken from the Holy Bible: Authorized King James Version. Copyright 1994. Published by Zondervan Publishing House, Grand Rapids, MI.

SCRIPTURE INDEX

1st Chronicles 16:34......Page 140

1st Corinthians 1:8......Page 192
1st Corinthians 2......Page 44 and 149
1st Corinthians 3 ......Page 45 and 101
1st Corinthians 6......Page 125 and 192
1st Corinthians 10......Page 49
1st Corinthians 12......Page 13, 42, 45, 190 and 192
1st Corinthians 13:4-8......Page 115
1st Corinthians 15......Page 133 and 192

1st John 1......Page 12, 21, and 191
1st John 2......Page 191
1st John 3......Page 28, 71, 182 and 192
1st John 4......Page 28 and 146
1st John 5......Page 71, 138 and 182

1st Peter 1......Page 35, 191 and 192
1st Peter 2......Page 21, 135, 143 and 191
1st Peter 3:18-22......Page 70
1st Peter 4......Page 45 and 166
1st Peter 5:8......Page 29 and 132

1st Samuel 15......Page 168
1st Samuel 16......Page 169
1st Samuel 17......Page 169
1st Samuel 18:7......Page 170
1st Samuel 31:4......Page 170

1st Thessalonians 5......Page 1, 14 and 196

1st Timothy......Page 167
1st Timothy 3:2-4......Page 110

2nd Chronicles 7:14......Page 195

2nd Corinthians 3:17......Page 181
2nd Corinthians 4:4......Page 28
2nd Corinthians 5......Page 21, 34, 40, 130 and 192
2nd Corinthians 6......Page 3, 8, 28 and 49
 2nd Corinthians 9:6-8......Page 190
2nd Corinthians 11:14......Page 28
2nd Corinthians 12:9......Page 103
2nd Corinthians 13:14......Page 42

2nd Kings 4......Page 183

2nd Thessalonians 2......Page 28
2nd Thessalonians 3:6......Page 65

2nd Timothy......Page 146, 147, 166 and 192
2nd Timothy 2......Page 146, 150, 166 and 190
2nd Timothy 3......Page 148
2nd Timothy 4......Page 191

2nd Peter 1:21......Page 148
2nd Peter 2:20......Page 189

2nd Samuel 11......Page 171 and 172
2nd Samuel 12:10-16......Page 171
2nd Samuel 15:6......Page 172

Acts 2:21......Page 136
Acts 3:15......Page 191
Acts 4......Page 136
Acts 5:3......Page 44
Acts 9:18......Page 55
Acts 10......Page 137 and 191
Acts 11:26......Page 192
Acts 14:9......Page 136
Acts 15:11......Page 191
Acts 16:17......Page 192
Acts 20:28......Page 128

Colossians 1......Page 12, 28, 128 and 193
Colossians 2:10......Page 193
Colossians 3:18-19.......Page 114

Daniel 8:9-11......Page 28

Deuteronomy 5:16......Page 146
Deuteronomy 11......Page 8, 51, 66 and 183
Deuteronomy 28......Page 27, 183, 184 and 185
Deuteronomy 31:6......Page 178

Ecclesiastes 3:1......Page 133
Ecclesiastes 9:9......Page 97

Ephesians 1......Page 45, 128, 191, 192 and 193
Ephesians 2......Page 28, 128, 136, 175, 191 and 192
Ephesians 4......Page 24, 44, 45 and 54
Ephesians 5......Page 86
Ephesians 6......Page 28, 29, 33, 35, 146 and 163

Exodus 3......Page 3
Exodus 12:22-23......Page 129
Exodus 15:26......Page 5 and 134
Exodus 17:15......Page 4
Exodus 20......Page 1, 2, 121 and 146

Ezekiel 28......Page 22 and 28
Ezekiel 48:35......Page 6

Galatians 2......Page 191
Galatians 3......Page 86 and 192
Galatians 4:28...... 192
Galatians 5......Page 29, 45, 167 and 179
Galatians 6:7......Page 50

Genesis 1......Page 7 and 83
Genesis 2......Page 88 and 114
Genesis 3:9......Page 84
Genesis 12:1-3......Page 37
Genesis 21:24......Page 86
Genesis 22:14......Page 4
Genesis 50......Page 14, 50, 65 and 78

Habakkuk 2:2......Page 182

Hebrews 3:1......Page 192
Hebrews 4:12......Page 35
Hebrews 9......Page 44 and 128
Hebrews 10......Page 45 and 128
Hebrews 11......Page 7, 34, 67, 134, 138 and 178
Hebrews 12:2......Page 191
Hebrews 13......Page 15, 49, 121, 128, 191 and 194

Hosea 4......Page 8, 10, 60, 67, 128, 166 and 193

Isaiah 4:4......Page 40 and 45
Isaiah 9:6......Page 191
Isaiah 11:2......Page 45
Isaiah 14......Page 22 and 28
Isaiah 26:3......Page 34
Isaiah 27:1......Page 28
Isaiah 28:10......Page 167
Isaiah 30......Page 71 and 133
Isaiah 35:4......Page 179
Isaiah 40......Page 133 and 194
Isaiah 53:5......Page 21 and 144
Isaiah 54:13......Page 47 and 163
Isaiah 55......Page 3, 47 and 91
Isaiah 64:6......Page 33

James 1......Page 2, 12, 14, 40, 49, 50, 64, 108 and 112
James 3:11......Page 8
James 4......Page 19, 31, 34, 35,129 and 144
James 5......Page 137

Jeremiah 7:23......Page 37
Jeremiah 23:6......Page 6
Jeremiah 29:11......Page 131, 142 and 144
Jeremiah 30:22......Page 37

Job 22:28......Page 182

Joel 2:25......Page 90

John 1......Page 29, 31, 191 and 193
John 2:13-16......Page 25
John 3......Page 20 and 128
John 5:24......Page 122
John 6:53-54......Page 101 and 128
John 8......Page 28, 135, 150, 179 and 191
John 10 ......Page 10, 19, 29, 36, 128 and 188

John 11:25......Page 191
John 12:31-32......Page 28
John 13......Page 15
John 14......Page 38, 43, 45, 69 and 191
John 15......Page 45, 182, 192 and 193
John 16:23-24......Page 38 and 69
John 17......Page 28 and 67
John 19......Page 21

Joshua 1:5......Page 6

Judges 6:24......Page 5

Leviticus 20:10......Page 121

Luke 1......Page 44, 90 and 191
Luke 4......Page 12 and 150
Luke 6......Page 59, 61, 67 and 188
Luke 12:7......Page 123
Luke 8:36......Page 136
Luke 9......Page 67 and 101
Luke 10 ......Page 10, 23, 129, 189 and 193

Luke 11......Page 28, 38, 45 and 69
Luke 12......Page 17, 125 and 171
Luke 14:26......Page 146
Luke 17......Page 18, 39, 63 and 134
Luke 18:42......Page 136
Luke 23:34......Page 66

Malachi 3:10......Page 188
Malachi 4:2......Page 191

Mark 1......Page 12, 28, 191 and 192
Mark 3......Page 50 and 118
Mark 5......Page101, 135 and 136
Mark 6:56......Page 101, 135 and 136
Mark 7:13......Page 59 and 163
Mark 9:42......Page 18
Mark 10 ......Page 18 and 187
Mark 14......Page 17 and 67
Mark 16......Page 136 and 137

Matthew 1:2......Page 191
Matthew 2:6......Page 191
Matthew 4......Page 12, and 28
Matthew 5......Page 27, 61, 120 and 192
Matthew 6...... Page 1, 15, 16, 17, 38, 69, 73, 88 and 186
Matthew 7......Page 38, 57, 59, 144 and 167
Matthew 8......Page 5
Matthew 10:30......Page 17 and 189
Matthew 12......Page 28, 44, 50 and 122
Matthew 13:39......Page 28

Matthew 14......Page 101
Matthew 16......Page 31 and 32
Matthew 17......Page 187
Matthew 18......Page 18, 29, 30, 39, 118 and 127
Matthew 19......Page 121
Matthew 21......Page 25 and 38
Matthew 25:21......Page 33
Matthew 26:53......Page 67
Matthew 28......Page 6, 11 and 42

Philippians 4......Page 34, 42, 78, 79, 92, 123 and 178

Proverbs 3...... Page 1, 5, 62 and 190
Proverbs 4:20-22......Page 70
Proverbs 6......Page 64
Proverbs 12:22......Page 64
Proverbs 13:24......Page 39
Proverbs 14:34......Page 6
Proverbs 18......Page 51, 141 and 182
Proverbs 21:19......Page 116
Proverbs 22:6......Page 164
Proverbs 29 ......Page 39 and 158
Proverbs 31......Page 113

Psalm 4:3......Page 192
Psalm 5......Page 79, 80 and 81
Psalm 7:17......Page 7
Psalm 12:2-3......Page 167
Psalm 23......Page 1, 73 and 74
Psalm 27:14......Page 133
Psalm 31:18......Page 64
Psalm 34:4......Page 179
Psalms 37......Page 72
Psalm 39:1......182

Psalm 46:10......Page 71 and 133
Psalm 47......Page 35 and 72
Psalm 51......Page 6, 51,173 and 174
Psalm 52:2-3......Page 63
Psalm 55:16......Page 196
Psalm 56......Page 81 and 82
Psalm 57......Page83
Psalm 91......Page 18, 75, 76, 77, 125 and 145

Psalm 103......Page 6, 134
Psalm 112......Page 110
Psalm 119:45......Page181
Psalm 120:2......Page 63
Psalm 127:3......Page85
Psalm 139:7-10......Page 44

Revelation 1......Page 128 and 191
Revelation 2:7......Page 42
Revelation 3......Page 25, 27, 39 and 191
Revelation 5:5......Page 191 and 193
Revelation 9......Page 28 and 29
Revelation 12......Page 11, 22, 28 and 128
Revelation 14:9-10......Page 28
Revelation 19:16......Page 191
Revelation 22:16......Page 191

Romans 1......Page 191 and 192
Romans 3......Page 61, 116, 127 and 177
Romans 4......Page 138, 182 and 183
Romans 5......Page 128, 133 and 191
Romans 6......Page192
Romans 8......Page 3, 42, 45, 122, 133 and 193
Romans 9:21......Page 124
Romans 10......Page 34, 40 and 135
Romans 12......Page 22, 45, 72 and 142
Romans 16:17-18......Page 64

Zechariah 4:10......Page 194

INDEX

"A Ready Defense" ...... Page 148
ABBA FATHER......Page 17, 124 and 193
ABEKA......Page 160
Abomination......Page 64
Abraham......Page 130
Abrahamic Covenant......Page 37
Absalom......Page 172
Adams, John......Page 32
Addictions......Page 152
Adonai......Page 8
Adonijah......Page 173

Allergists......Page 98
Alternative Health......Page 102
Amazon.com......Page 162
"American Heritage Teaching Series" ......Page 160
Amnon......Page 172
Anchell, Dr. Melvin......Page 164
"And the Bride Wore White" ....Page 164
Andropause......Page 96 and 97
Angels......Page 6, 18, 54 and 145
Anger......Page 24
Anointing of the Holy Spirit......Page 44
Anointing Oil......Page 137, 154 and 155

Anti-aging Doctors......Page 98
Antichrist......Page 28
Apple of His Eye......Page 17
Armour Bearer......Page 169
Armour of God......Page 33
Artificial Hormone Replacement Therapy......Page 99
Atheists/Agnostics......Page 55
Authority......Page 11 and 30

Baby Steps......Page 66, 109, 186 and 194
Baptized In the Holy Spirit......Page 42-45
Barley Bread......Page 99
Barton, David......Page 160
Basham, Don......Page 46
Bathsheba......Page 171

"Ben Hur: A Tale of the Christ"......Page 57
Bennett, Dennis and Rita......Page 43 and 45
Biblical Discipline......Page 38, 39, 85, 156 and 157
Biblical Headship......Page 86
*"Biblical Mathematics, Key to Scripture Numerics:
How to Count the Bible"*......Page 170
Binding and Loosening......Page 118 and 119
Bioidenticals......Page 99
Bishop......Page 110

205

Blame Out......Page 12
Blasphemy......Page 166
Blasphemy of the Holy Spirit......Page 50 and 52
Blessing Blocker......Page 139, 187 and 188
Blessing, Car or House......Page 156
Blessing the Next Generation" ......Page 20, 130 and 132
Blessings and Curses......Page 181
Blood Brought......Page 20 and 21
Blood Guiltiness......Page 176
Blood of Jesus......Page 127, 128, 129, 130, 131 and 132
Bloody...... Page 80

Bond Servant......Page 8
Bondage......Page 178, 180 and 183
Born Again Experience......Page 20
Boston Massacre......Page 32
Boundaries......Page 158
Bowling, Pastor Sarah......Page 20, 130 and 131
Breastplate of Righteousness......Page 33
Bright Morning Star......Page 22
Brim, Pastor Billye......Page 22 and 129
Broer, Dr. Ted (Sharon)......Page 102
Bullinger, Dr. E. W......Page 8
Burke, Edmund......Page 26
By His Stripes......Page 21

California......Page 178
Calvary......Page 20, 130 and 136
"Cat's In the Cradle".......Page 87
Chapin, Harry, Sandy......Page 87
Characteristics of the Holy Spirit......Page 42
Charity......Page 115
Children......Page 18, 85 and 141
Christian Counselors......Page 94, 95 and 105
Church Board of Directors......Page 187
Church of the Laodiceans......Page 25
City of Ai......Page 4

Colbert, Dr, Don (Mary)......Page 102
Communication......Page 88
"Companion Bible, The"......Page 8
Confession of Faith......Page 31, 32, 131, 138 and 185
Costa, Jr., Dr. Robert...Page 3
Counseling......Page 94
Crisis Christian......Page 2
Crucifying Christ......Page 92
Curse of Death......Page 35
Curses......Page 35, 117, 118, 140, 141, 142 and 153

Daly, Mr. James......Page 104
"Dateable: Are You? Are They?".......Page 164
David, King......Page 168, 169 and 170
Davis, June Newman......Page 143

Day Care Centers......Page 86 and 87
Demaria, Dr. Bob......Page 100
Demons......Page 33 and 53
DeMoss, Nancy Leigh......Page 164
Destiny School of Ministry......Page 119

Diabetes......Page 97
Difference Makers......Page 27
Divorce......89, 90, 94, and 122
Do The Wicker Prosper......Page 72
Dobson, Dr. James......Page 105
Dominion......Page 30, 85 and 185
"Don't Worry, Be Happy"......Page 178
"Dr. Bob's Transat Survival Guide"......Page 102

Elect of God......Page 52
Elisha, Prophet......Page 183 and 184
End Times......Page 52
Err......Page 112
Evangel Christian Church......Page 119
Ezra......Page 147

Facts......Page 31 and 32
False gods......Page 1
Family......Page 85 and 86
Fannin, Larry and Sun......Page 186
Fasting......Page 186
Father of all lies......Page 12
Fear/Worry......Page 178, 179 and 180

Fixed......Page 111
Flour......Page 100 and 101
Flying J......Page 181
Focus on the Family Ministries......Page 105
Forgiveness......Page 59, 60, 61, 62, 66 and 168-177
Free Will Choices......Page 8 and 183
Fruit of the Spirit......Page 45 and 167

Garden of Eden......Page 35 and 122
Garden of Gethsemane......Page 17, 67 and 131
Gay, Robert......Page 36
Gifts of The Spirit, groups, purpose......Page 45
Girdle of Truth......Page 33
God cannot do evil......Page 12
God Communicates......Page 19
Goliath......Page 169 and 170

Good Shepherd......Page 19
Gospel of Truth......Page 33
Greens......Page 101
Gresh, Dannah......Page 164
Grocery Shopping......Page 125
Grumpy Old Men Syndrome......Page 96
Guardian Angel......Page 18

Hagen, Pastor Kenneth E.......Page 10 and 11
"Hand That Rocks the Cradle"......Page 87
Hardened Heart......Page 66
Healing......Page 135
Heart Disease......Page 97
Hearts of Stone......Page 60
Hedge of Protection......Page 127 and 145
Helmet of Salvation......Page 34

Hickey, Pastor Marilyn......Page 8, 20, 130 and 131
Holy Spirit......Page 42, 50, 52, 55, 56 and 93
"Holy Spirit Baptism"......Page 46
"Holy Spirit Today"......Page 45
Home Schoolers......Page 160
Homologia......Page 32
Hormones......Page 96, 98, 99 and 160
Hosts of God......Page 6
How God views prayer......Page 67
"How to Speak Your Spouse's Language"......Page 105
Hyssop......Page 129 and 174

I AM THAT I AM......Page 3
"If My People, A Guide on Fasting and Prayer"......Page 186
Ingersoll, Robert G......Page 56
Iniquities......Page 134
Intercessory Prayer......Page 31
Israelites......Page 121 and 130
"I Surrender All"......Page 61

Jehovah Names of God......Page 4, 5, 6, 94, 103 and 188
Jesse, the Bethlehemite......Page 168
Jesus as our Saviour......Page 20 and 43
Jesus feeding the 4000......Page 102
Jesus feeding the 5000......Page 101 and 102
Jesus prayed to His Father......Page 67
Jesus spoke six times from the Cross......Page 21 and 66
Judgment......Page 56
Joab......Page 171 and 172

King James Bible......Page 142 and 149

Law of Gravity......Page 96
Leasing......Page 80
"Lies Young Women Believe"......Page 164
Life Bible College......Page 126
Life Changes......Page 96
Lincoln, Abraham......Page 161
Lookadoo, Justin......Page 164
LORD......Page 4
Louisiana......Page 178
Love Bugs......Page 180

Lucifer......Page 22 and 30
Lucado, Max......Page 73
Lucre......Page 110
Lying......Page 63, 64 and 65

Maine......Page 178
Man's Free Will Choice......Page 58
Manipulation and Witchcraft......Page 120 and 168
Marriage......Page 92, 93, 97, 99, 104, 109 and 121
Marriage Vows......Page 97 and 119
Masar......Page 147
Massorah......Page 147 and 148
Massorities......Page 147

McDowell, Josh......Page 148
McFerrin, Bobby......Page 178
Melt......Page 111
Men/Fathers/Husbands......Page 85, 86, 87, 88 and 109
Menopause......Page 96
Mid-Life Crisis......Page 97
Ministers......Page 166
Mocking God......Page 50
Money Changers in Temple......Page 25
Morgan, Hayley......Page 164
Moses......Page 121
Murray, Pastor Arnold......Page 25
Mystery of the Trinity.....Page 189

Names of Satan......Page 24 and 28
Natchez Trace......Page 180
Nathan, Prophet......Page 170 and 173
Nature of God......Page 3 and 8
Negative Emotions......Page 24, 25 and 179
Nehemiah......Page 147
Niagara Falls......Page 180
Number Five......Page 170
Nutrition......Page 100

"One Night with the King"......Page 168
Oregano......Page 174
Osborn, Dr. T. L. ......Page 135 and 136
Our Shield of Faith......Page 34

Pagan Altars......Page 1
Pandora's Box......Page 122
Passover......Page 152
Perimenopause......Page 96
Personal relationship with God......Page 2, 6, 16, 19 and 53
Petra......Page 31
Petros......Page 31
Philistine......Page 167
Physical Therapy......Page 98
Piscopo, Dr. Sherill......Page 119

Planned Parenthood......Page 161
Poor Me Baby…...Page 49
Prairie Dogs…...Page 178
Praise Music......Page 141
Praising God......Page 30
Prayer, Intercessory......Page 31
Prayer/Praying......Page 16, 37, 69, 70, 71, 73, 122,123, 132, 179 and 193
Prayer of Salvation......Page 195
Prayer, Warfare......Page 31
Praying Over Serious Situations…...Page 78 and 134

Precious Metals......Page 40
Primm, Nevada......Page 180
Prince, Derek......Page 36
Priorities......Page 1 and 87 and 88
Profession of Faith......Page 60, 94, 183, 184 and 185
Psalm of Protection......Page 75

Rapture Theory......Page 53
Rejoice In the LORD Always......Page 78
Relationships:
    Fast Food......Page 16
    Full Custody......Page 16
    Personal......Page 16, 53, 67, 78, 147, 179 and 192
    Visitation......Page 16
Righteous Indignation......Page 26
Righteousness......Page 6
Robert Costa Ministries......Page 3
Rote Recitations......Page 17
Rubin, Dr. Jordan S......Page 102

Sacred Hebrew Word......Page 3
Sacrifice of Praise......Page 15
"Safe in the Shepherd's Arms"......Page 73
Salvation......Page 33, 52, 53, 130, 135 and 177
Salvation Prayer......Page 195
Samuel, Prophet......Page 168 and 169
Saphar......Page 147

Satan......Page 22, 28, 29, 54, 85, 88, 122, 127, 134, 141, 156, 178 and 183
Satan's Names......Page 28
Satan's Goals and Purposes......Page 10 and 128
Satan's Five "I Will" statements......Page 22
Satan's Tactics......Page 10, 70 and 151
Satan's Nature......Page 22
Satan's Punishment......Page 30
Satan's Roles......Page 29
Satan trying to tempt Jesus......Page 12

Saul, King......Page 168, 169, 170 and 171
Saxion, Dr. Valerie......Page 102
Scott, Dr. Dick ......Page 128
Scorpions......Page 10
"Scripture Keys for Kingdom Living"…..Page 143

Selah......Page 63, 83 and 84
Seed......Page 110
Sepulcher......Page 80
Serpents......Page 10
Servant's Heart......Page 15
Seven Deadly Sins......Page 29
Sex......Page 85, 122 and 164
"Sexy Girls: How Hot is Too Hot?"......Page 161
Sexually Transmitted Diseases......Page 85

Shepherd, J.W.......Page 21
Shepherd's Chapel......Page 25
Shoes of the Preparation of the Gospel of Peace......Page 34
Shunammite Woman......Page 183
"Silencing the Enemy"......Page 30
Singing......Page 35
Smelting Fire......Page 40 and 78
Smelting Pot......Page 40
Society......Page 85
Solomon, King......Page 172 and 173
Songs of Praise......Page 35
Sopherim......Page 147

Speaking In Tongues......Page 42-44
Spirit of Burning......Page 40 and 45
Spiritual Gifting......Page 45
"Spiritual Warfare"......Page 36
Spiritual Warfare......Page 30, 31, 35, 36 and 70
Spoil......Page 113
Spouses......Page 88

Statement of Faith......Page 166
Star Wars......Page 23
Statement of Faith......Page 164
Strobel, Lee......Page 56
"Strong's Exhaustive Concordance"......Page 102, 142, 147 and 149
Strongholds......Page 151, 152 and 187
Suffer......Page 129
Sumrall, Dr. Lester......Page 30, 122, 178, 179, 185 and 189
Sword of the Spirit......Page 35

T-Rex......Page 180
"Take It...It's Yours, Seizing Your Spiritual Dominion" ......Page 30, 122, 178, 185 and 189
Tamar......Page 172
Teens and Preteens......Page 158- 165
Tetelestai......Page 21
Ten Commandments......Page 27
Testosterone......Page 96

"The Believer's Authority"......Page 10 and 11
"The Blood and the Glory"......Page 22 and 129
"The Case for Christ"......Page 56
"The Christ of the Gospels"......Page 21
The Devil......Page 8 and Page 30
The Devil Made Me Do It......Page 12
"The Divine Names and Titles"......Page 8
The Five "I Will's"......Page 22
"The Holy Spirit and You"......Page 43
The LORD Is My Shepherd......Page 74

"The Makers Diet"......Page 102
"The Marriage Checkup"......Page 105
"The Names of God"......Page 8
The Our Father......Page 73
"The Secret Keeper: The Delicate Power of Modesty"......Page 164
"The Seven Pillars of Health"......Page 102
"The Technical Virgin: How Far is too Far?".......Page 164
The Tetragrammaton...... Page 3
The Vision......Page 180

Time Wasters......Page 54
Tithing......Page 188 and 189
"To Sit at the Right Hand"......Page 11
Traditional Morals, Values......Page 85, 87 and 101
Traditions of Men......Page 59, 161 and 187
Traveling Mercies......Page 125
Trials and Tribulations......Page 47
Trinity Broadcasting Network...Page 102
Tumble Weeds......Page 178
Twelve Disciples......Page 15, 103 and 187
Types of Prayer......Pages 31

Unforgiveable Sin......Page 50 and 122
Uriah the Hittite......Page 171

Vain Repetitions......Page 17
Vallowe, Ed F......Page 170
Verb Tense of Petros and Petra......Page 31 and 32
Vessel of Dishonour......Page 66
Virginity......Page 85 and 163

Wagner, C. Peter......Page 36 and 45
Wallace, General William Ross......Page 87
Wallace, General Lew......Page 57
Warfare Prayer......Page 31
"What's Wrong With Sex Education?"......Page 164
"What's Wrong With Sex Education?
Preteen and Teenage Sexual Development and Environmental Influences"......Page 164

Who is God......Page 189
Who are we in Christ Jesus......Page 190 and 191
Why Do We Pray......Page 67 and 191
Wicked People......Page 72

Wilderness......Page 38 and 121
Wilson, Bill......Page 149
WMCA......Page 160
Women / Wives......Page 85, 86, 88 and 109
Wright, Dr. H. Norman......Page 105

YAHWEH......Page 3
"Your Spiritual Gifts"......Page 45

Zadok, Priest......Page 173

www.ingramcontent.com/pod-product-compliance
Lightning Source LLC
Chambersburg PA
CBHW032250150426
43195CB00008BA/395